Series

THE AMERICAN ANGLER GUIDE TO

FLY FISHING FOR TROUT

PROVEN SKILLS, TECHNIQUES, AND TACTICS FROM THE PROS

AARON JASPER

LYONS PRESS
GUILFORD, CONNECTICUT
An Imprint Of Globe Pequot Press

Lyons Press is an imprint of Globe Pequot Press.

Project editor: Staci Zacharski
Text design: Sheryl Kober
Layout artist: Sue Murray

Library of Congress Cataloging-in-Publication data is available on file.

ISBN 978-0-7627-8808-8

Printed in the United States of America

10 9 8 7 6 5 4 3 2 1

CONTENTS

FOREWORD
By Simon Gawesworth

There are many reasons people go fly-fishing: For some, it's a chance to get away from it all; some go to be with their buddies; others go fishing to enjoy the natural world; and there are plenty of anglers who go fishing just to catch fish! You can fly-fish for steelhead, salmon, trout, bass, carp, pike, bonefish, tarpon, dorado, and a hundred other species, and each species has its aficionados and dedicated disciples.

I am a purist only in that I will do nothing but fly-fish. I honestly don't mind if I am fly-fishing for a trout, a steelhead, a bonefish, or a carp; it is the act of fly-fishing and fly-casting that I enjoy, and that I have fallen passionately in love with since my dad started teaching me back in the early 1970s.

For other folk, a certain species can become an obsession. I have fly-fishing friends who spend a fortune every year going to the best lodges in British Columbia to fish for steelhead, pooh-poohing their local trout waters. Perhaps even worse (read, expensive), I have many friends who travel the world in search of Atlantic salmon, frequenting hallowed rivers in Norway, Iceland, Russia, and Scotland. To these folk, there are no other species worth fly-fishing for; the species has become their obsession.

One such person is Aaron Jasper. I met Aaron several years ago at a fly-fishing show in New Jersey, and the first thing that struck me about him was his passion for fly-fishing for trout. Aaron has been fly-fishing since the age of seven and has spent hundreds and thousands of hours pursuing this noble, yet fickle, creature. He has an insatiable appetite to learn new things and has studied and mastered every possible way known to man to catch a trout on a fly rod.

Never afraid to try something new, and to break the boundaries of traditional fly-fishing methods, Aaron's mission is quite simple: to find better and more-effective ways to catch lots of trout. This hunger for success has led Aaron to master skills rarely seen in the United States—skills such as European nymphing, traditional wet-fly fishing, and "Loch-style" fishing on a lake. These newer additions to his armory, strengthened by his many years of experience with "normal" fly-fishing tactics with dry flies, streamers, and nymphs, has produced one of the most effective and deadliest trout anglers I know.

It is of great benefit to the fly-fishing world that Aaron has put pen to paper, sharing many of the things he has learned in this book. From anglers who are just getting started fly-fishing for trout, to highly accomplished, seasoned veterans of the fly, this book will be an invaluable asset for all, packed full of tips and information designed to help you catch more trout.

INTRODUCTION

The objective of this book is to enable beginning or intermediate fly fishers to pursue various kinds of trout. It will outline the tactics that are needed to catch trout in various fishable watersheds.

As a fly fisher, you are on a journey—one that will ultimately encompass a great deal of skill and knowledge. This book is not for the angler who knows everything. Instead, it's meant for the angler who is progressing through the sport and needs guidance on how to make decisions regarding tackle, leaders, and the varying types of water he or she will face on each trip.

This book is written in approximately the same way in which I made my fly-fishing journey. First, I learned the various types of nymphing. From there I went to dry flies. After that I made the crossover to fishing dry/dropper systems. Once I became proficient with these techniques, I branched out and learned more-advanced tactics, such as how to use wet flies, fish still water, and night-fish. The latter is the ultimate in fly fishing. When night-fishing for trophy trout, you are truly stalking your quarry. You are alone in the darkness, unable to see what is in front of you.

Take what I've written in this book, study it, practice it, and master the techniques from the beginning. All of the foundations, concepts, and riggings are laid out clearly and concisely. All that's left is for you to make a trip to the stream.

A young, potential fly fisher watches as the author lands a trout in a small stream. Capturing the interest of new fly fishers is one of the author's genuine interests.
HEATH POTTER

CHAPTER 1

The Fish

There are four main species of trout that fly fishers pursue here in the United States: brook, brown, cutthroat, and rainbow trout. All four species have many subspecies, which can be found throughout the country. All but one is native to the United States. The brown trout is of European origin. All four of the species lend themselves to being caught with a fly rod.

The author is holding a perfectly colored brown trout.
HEATH POTTER

1

As the "holy grail" of angling for fish in freshwater, fly-fishing for trout takes you to some of the most beautiful places on the planet. Due to the fact that the trout need cold, clean water, the habitats in which they live are generally pristine. Within the waters I discuss, there are three types of fisheries. *Wild fisheries* are streams wherein the fish have self-sustaining populations. *Put-and-take fisheries,* by contrast, are stocked and cannot typically sustain wild fish. Waters that are a combination of both are called *trout-maintenance fisheries,* where some wild fish are found, but not enough to sustain a sport fishery. These fisheries need additional stocking to help bolster the population. Fisheries can be native or indigenous, wild and native, invasive and wild, stocked, holdover, or some combination.

BROOK TROUT

Brookies are actually classified as char rather than trout, which puts them in the same class as lake, bull, and Dolly Varden trout. The brook trout is the state fish for Michigan, New Hampshire, New Jersey, New York, Pennsylvania, Vermont, Virginia, and West Virginia. This also correlates with the brook trout's native range, which is the Appalachian Mountains, as well as much of eastern Canada. Brook trout are typically found in the headwater sections of streams.

Brook trout originated in the East but were brought out west and stocked in many rivers and lakes, becoming quite prolific due to the ideal growing conditions in the West. As an invasive species in many Western rivers, they have displaced other native trout species. Brook trout thrive in colder water, present in headwater streams, much like all the other species of char. They prefer water temperatures that range anywhere from 32 to 72 degrees Fahrenheit and can become stressed once the water temperature reaches 65 degrees. Brook trout are fancied as a fly-rod fish because they are extremely aggressive. High headwater streams tend to be fairly acidic, which does not lend itself to prolific insect activity. This makes brookies fairly opportunistic.

The author fishes a small brook trout stream. These streams are commonly found in the Mid-Atlantic and Northeast. Here, he's landing a nice wild brookie taken on a PMX dry fly. KELLY BUCHTA

An average-size wild brook trout from a northeastern stream. AARON JASPER

Brook trout habitat is being rapidly reduced due in large part to man's impact on the waterways. The fish is sensitive to poor oxygen levels in rivers, pollution, and changes in pH caused by environmental effects. The logging industry in the Northeast and Mid-Atlantic has led to decreased canopy over the streams, increasing the water temperatures throughout much of the brook trout's native range. In addition, land left unplanted, where sediment and silt can easily be carried into the stream, adds heavy sediment loads to the streams. Therefore, macroinvertebrate habitat is being lost due to the rock in the streambed being covered by silt and debris.

Brook trout are the smallest of the major trout species. An average brook trout in a small mountain stream might only be four to eight inches long. A large brook trout, such as one that might be caught in Labrador, might exceed twenty-four inches and weigh over eight pounds. Fish of that size are rare, however, because brook trout do not live very long.

The largest wild brook trout currently found in the United States are in the Rapid River in Maine, as well as a few other select remote streams in that same state. Because they reproduce in the fall, and their native range is known for harsh winters, in-stream freezing during the winter months adds up to lower survival of juvenile brook trout. When compared with other species of trout, all of this means lower spawning success and a shorter life span (generally four to five years, which is quite short).

Brook trout are easy to catch on a fly rod. The lack of food found in their typical headwater streams makes them very opportunistic and susceptible to being caught on dry flies. Despite the size of the fish, seeing them rise to a dry fly can be quite exciting. Some of the fish are so small that the flies they are attempting to eat are larger than they are. In the Northeast there are many anglers whose only desire is to catch wild brook trout in high-gradient freestone streams. There are excellent populations of brook trout in the Smoky Mountains, West Virginia, Pennsylvania, the Adirondacks, New Jersey, Massachusetts, Vermont, New Hampshire, and Maine. There are also smaller pockets of indigenous populations of brook trout in other states in the Mid-Atlantic and Northeast.

BROWN TROUT

Brown trout are an invasive species in the United States. Originally from Europe, they were brought here in the 1800s, first planted as a sport fish in various rivers in the Northeast. Brown trout have displaced brook trout to a great degree throughout the entire Mid-Atlantic and Northeast regions. They are a very desirable fly-rod species because of their elusiveness and selectivity. Many fly anglers consider catching a brown trout in excess of thirty inches on a fly to be the greatest accomplishment in the sport of fly fishing.

Brown trout reach massive sizes and can weigh in excess of ten pounds. They've been introduced to forty-five of the fifty states, and self-sustaining populations have been found in thirty-four of them.

The Fario-strain brown trout is indigenous to certain parts of Europe. Locals commonly refer them to as zebra trout or Adidas trout. AARON JASPER

Large, low-gradient rivers, such as the Missouri River in Montana, are ideally suited for indicator nymphing. Here is a twenty-seven-inch wild brown trout taken on a caddis larva by the author. BOB CARPENTER

These fish are also able to survive and thrive in warmer water temperatures than most trout species indigenous to the United States. As a result, in areas where brown trout have been introduced, they have overtaken other species that were once native to the area. New York State, for instance, has seen a drastic decline in brook trout populations due in part to the introduction of brown trout.

In some regions where they have access to cool salt water, they can also become anadromous. This means that they spend the majority of their time at sea but come back to freshwater rivers to spawn. These brown trout, when they come into freshwater, can be very silvery and weigh in excess of twenty pounds. Connecticut has a very popular sea-run brown trout fishery along its Long Island Sound coastline.

Brown trout can tolerate water temperatures anywhere from 32 degrees Fahrenheit all the way up into the 80s, provided that the oxygen saturation in the water is sufficient. This means that they can commonly be found in high-gradient streams where the water is very turbulent or where there are cool springs that enter the river. In addition to living in the same turbulent environments where native species thrive, they can also be found in larger US rivers and streams. These trout also thrive in tailwater river systems. The majority of tailwater systems found throughout the United States contain large populations of stocked, wild, and holdover brown trout.

Brown trout reach maturity in three to four years. They spawn from September all the way through to early January, depending on the region. When hatched, juvenile brown trout feed on insects and other invertebrates. However, as they grow they become predatory and start to eat other fish, often including their own young. A brown trout grows larger than other trout in part because of its ability to switch food sources.

Brown trout are highly valuable to anglers as a sport fish. They are everything a fly-rod quarry should be: beautiful, elusive, selective, and alert to their surroundings, especially when found in spring creeks. Since they grow quite large, fly anglers can target browns of varying sizes, using a wide array of techniques, from dry flies to large streamers. Interestingly, the two largest browns on record were caught in the United States, despite being out of their native range. Both were in excess of forty pounds. They have yet to be caught, giving fly fishers hope that they might be able to catch a fish near this size. The largest wild brown trout that I know of, caught with a fly rod, came out of the Norfork River in Arkansas. It weighed in at almost thirty-eight pounds.

CUTTHROAT TROUT

The cutthroat trout's native ranges include all of the major Pacific Coast drainages, from Prince William Sound in Alaska down to northern California. Other sustained populations are found throughout the Rocky Mountains and east to the Hudson Bay in Canada, as well as rivers in the Mississippi River drainage and Pacific basins, from southern Alberta to the Rio Grande River drainage in New Mexico. However, with the introduction of nonnative species, their ranges have become severely

The author holds an average-size Yellowstone River cutthroat trout taken from the Yellowstone River, right below Yellowstone Lake. HEATH POTTER

Montana's Yellowstone River (seen here, below Yellowstone Lake) was once the last stronghold of indigenous Yellowstone cutthroat trout. AARON JASPER

compromised. Cutthroat trout have also been stocked in many locations throughout the United States outside of their native range, including the White River below Bull Shoals Dam and in the Norfork River in Arkansas. They are also found in Montana, Minnesota, Nebraska, Nevada, New Jersey, Virginia, and West Virginia. Stocking of cutthroat trout worked in Arizona, California, Colorado, Montana, Nevada, and Utah, according to the US Geological Survey (USGS). In all of the other states where stocking was attempted, it has either been ceased or has become a put-and-take fishery.

Cutthroats are susceptible to changes within their environment and require pristine habitat in order to survive. Much like brook trout, they require high-quality, cold water, and thus are often found at higher elevations. The introduction of rainbow, brook, and brown trout into the Western United States has been a major detriment to cutthroat populations. Rainbows and browns both predate on cutthroat eggs and young. Cutthroat trout are less aggressive by nature and are often outcompeted by other trout species.

According to Trout Unlimited, the Colorado River cutthroat is found in only 16 percent of the watersheds that are in its historic range. The Lahontan cutthroat trout, the largest subspecies, has reached weights in excess of twenty pounds; the current species world record, at forty-one pounds, was caught in Pyramid Lake in Nevada. Damming rivers and cutting them off from spawning habitat has led to the decline of the Lahontan cutthroat. Since damming the Truckee River, they have been stocked in Pyramid Lake and are thriving. Mike Sexton, a member of the Fly Fishing Team USA, reports that a twenty-four-pound Lahontan cutthroat was caught there last year by someone not using a fly rod. Additionally, the Yellowstone cutthroat trout is endangered in its native range. Lake trout have been introduced into Yellowstone Lake and are causing cutthroat numbers to decline rapidly.

Where cutthroat still have a stronghold, they provide fly anglers with exceptional opportunities. Cutthroats, like brook trout, are extremely opportunistic and take dry flies very well. Cutthroat trout prefer the same areas as brook trout in the West, such as high mountain streams and lakes where the biomass of available food is not very abundant. Most of their feeding takes place from June through October, due to harsh winters and the ensuing snowmelt. This is why many anglers come to Yellowstone National Park during the summer months, where some of the most famous cutthroat streams are found. The Yellowstone River holds some of the largest cutthroat trout in the West. Although their numbers are greatly diminished, an angler still has a decent chance of catching a trophy cutthroat trout of up to two feet in length.

In Colorado's Rocky Mountain National Park, the US Fish and Wildlife Service is bringing back the greenback cutthroat trout. These are mainly very small fish found in high-gradient freestone rivers within the park, as well as some high mountain lakes. These trout are very easy to catch and will readily take dry flies.

Pete Erickson, a guide and former member of the Fly Fishing Team USA, states, "The Snake River finespot cutthroat is perhaps my favorite trout species in the world. Although almost genetically identical to a Yellowstone cutthroat, they look totally different to any angler that catches one. They have orangish to red fins, and a silvery-purplish body, with a bold yellow belly when they get big . . . The body also has tiny, fine black spots." Fly fishers come from all over the world to catch these finespot cutts in the Snake River, where they are native and wild. Almost exclusive to the Jackson Hole area, they are strong fighters, and they get huge.

RAINBOW TROUT

Rainbow trout, like browns, are invasive to many watersheds throughout the United States. Unlike browns, however, rainbow trout originated in the United States. Their native range is the Pacific Coast of North America, from Alaska down to southern California. Rainbows can also become anadromous and go into salt water for part of their lifetimes. These fish are known as steelhead.

Rainbow trout are extremely temperature-tolerant, able to adapt to varying conditions—anywhere from 32 to 87 degrees Fahrenheit, given optimum dissolved-oxygen content in the stream. These fish are easily raised in hatcheries and stocked in nearly every state in the United States. Many anglers consider rainbows to be the most aggressive of all trout. They are almost like eating machines.

On a recent trip to Vermont, I fished a high mountain stream, which, according to the guide, once held only wild brook trout. But I caught at least five rainbow trout to every brookie. The guide said that once the state started stocking rainbow trout in the Otter River, the rainbows quickly moved up into the cooler tributaries during the warmer summer months and started to reproduce on their own. If one were to look at a map of the United States that shows where rainbow trout are exotic, they would see that nearly the entire country east of Idaho (including most of Canada) has documented populations. Even Hawaii has a small wild population!

These days, however, even in states like Montana (where rainbows were once a dominant species), whirling disease, is caused by a tiny parasite, which is ingested by young trout, particularly rainbow trout, causing them to have weakened spines has killed many young each year. This forced US Fish and Wildlife to find whirling disease–resistant strains of the trout. In addition to Montana, many other Western states have had problems with whirling disease. As a result, US Fish and Wildlife has stocked rainbows in a number of Western rivers.

Rainbow trout are highly sought after by anglers. Famous for their acrobatic runs, rainbows tend to inhabit the faster sections of streams, making them strong fish. They can be caught with virtually any type of fly fishing: dry flies, nymphs, wet flies, and streamers. They also inhabit many different river zones and can be found in high-gradient mountain streams as well as low-gradient meadow runs. Rainbow trout are also found in high densities in lakes throughout the West. At one time, many Western states used airplanes to stock high mountain lakes. Many of these populations survive to this day.

TROUT BEHAVIOR

Now that we have looked into the four main species of trout found in the United States, it is important to understand a bit about their behavior. Since trout are cold-blooded, their activity is mainly based upon water temperatures. When the water is cold (under 40°F), trout can be very lethargic and only feed when there is an abundant food supply available. Conversely, as water temperatures increase, up to 68 degrees (or 60°F for brook trout), they become quite active and will feed with more aggression. They will also seek out those areas within a stream where they can have their oxygen needs met. When the water temperature gets into the low to mid-60s, all trout will position themselves in very turbulent water, where there is lots of oxygenated water created by the cascades and riffles. This is why we see trout in the faster-moving water during the spring, summer, and early fall, and why we see them move out of this type of water during the late fall into the winter months. This migration is cyclical, and is the same year after year.

The average trout for which we fly-fish (eight to eighteen inches) is not a predator. They are not actively seeking out food items such as small fish, crayfish, and smaller trout, but rather are positioning themselves in what we call *feeding lies*—those areas where they can safely feed on macroinvertebrates while maintaining the proper level of oxygen to sustain them. Occasionally, brown trout at the upper end of this size range can become quite predatory. Many of the tactics found in this book will not only catch the average trout but also the fish of a lifetime.

CHAPTER 2

The Casts

In fly fishing, casting is of the utmost importance. I always tell clients, "If you can't cast, you can't catch them."

I was fortunate to learn how to fly-cast at a very early age. When I was five I was at a fishing show in Rockland County, New York, where the famed Lefty Kreh was doing a casting demonstration. When he was finished, a family member went up to him and asked if he could show me a few things. After some very sloppy casting for the first twenty minutes—I'm

The author makes a proper forward cast. Notice the nice tight loop in front of him.
JUSIN IDE

sure he was quite frustrated—I began to properly create what I now know as the back-and-forward casting stroke. He worked with me for a good hour that day and gave me a good foundation from which to begin my casting. I tell people I was in the right place at the right time.

There are three things that will enable a fly caster to become proficient: Standing up straight and tall is the first one (trying to create power by lunging forward can only hinder your ability to properly cast a fly); breaking your wrist is the second (your rod should not travel in an arc, but rather a straight line); and keeping your casting stroke to the ten o'clock and two o'clock positions. The rod needs to stop in those positions in order to create the proper forward and backward casts, which are essential to delivering your flies.

Here you can see the hand positioning on the fly rod. Unless you are making a cast or are controlling the line in your other hand, keep the fly line under your front two fingers. This will make it easier to find the line when you need to manipulate it. JUSTIN IDE

Since fly fishing involves lures with little or no weight, the ability to throw them long distances requires some understanding of the basic principles of casting. Unlike spin fishing, where the weight of your lure enables you to cast, in fly fishing it's the weight of your line that gets the fly to where you want it to be.

THE BASIC CAST

When standing to make the cast, position your body upright and your shoulders square to the target. Slumping down, leaning, or lunging—which most people believe will help their cast, because those stances are all associated with power—will actually do more harm than good.

Once you are standing in an upright position, get your elbow as close to your side as possible—although you don't necessarily have to tuck your elbow in. Casting is not supposed to feel unnatural; you want to feel comfortable. Once you've found a relaxed position for your elbow, you're ready to cast.

Pull off about thirty feet of line and get it in front of you. To begin your cast, position the rod at two o'clock, almost at a 45-degree angle in front of you. Start to lift the rod sideways across your body. As you lift the rod, make sure to keep your wrist firm. As you begin your casting stroke, start slowly. Once the rod gets to one o'clock, start to accelerate the rod back until you reach the ten o'clock position behind you. Come to a complete stop at ten o'clock. Keep your wrist locked. Allowing your wrist to break can cause your loop to open up, preventing you from properly loading the rod for the forward cast. When beginning this, it is okay to watch your fly line behind you. What you want is for your fly line to become completely unrolled in a straight line at the end of the backcast. When this happens, begin your forward cast.

For the forward cast, start at ten o'clock. As you come to eleven o'clock, begin to accelerate the rod until you reach the two o'clock position; when you do, come to an abrupt stop. The harder the stop, the more the rod loads. You will see that the line moves so fast, it will tug on your hand when you make that stop.

Let the line fully roll out behind you or in front of you. If you hear a "whip crack," you are not letting your line play out enough. Great casting is really about clean, sharp movement. Accelerate, stop; accelerate, stop. Let the rod do the work, keep your movements precise, and keep the rod straight with your forearm. Ninety percent of a good cast is keeping these things in mind.

Remember that you don't want the rod to go in a circular motion; you want it to move as if it's on a sliding rail. Your hand should travel parallel to the ground throughout the entire casting stroke. Anytime your hand is raised or lowered, you break this plane and lose energy. If done properly, when you pick up the line, the rod will be under intense load. Even the fastest rod will flex when you pick up the line. When beginning the forward cast, much like the backcast, you will notice that the rod is under intense flex at the beginning. Accelerating the rod throughout the casting stroke loads the rod and creates the powerful forward cast.

Begin the forward cast when the line is straight out from your position.
ALEJANDRO GOMEZ

Bring the rod behind you to the ten o'clock position. Remember to accelerate the rod through the casting stroke. ALEJANDRO GOMEZ

Once the rod reaches this position, allow the loop to straighten out. ALEJANDRO GOMEZ

Once the loop unravels, begin your forward casting stroke. Again, remember to accelerate the rod the same way you would on the backcast. ALEJANDRO GOMEZ

Keep the rod tip up high as the cast unravels in front of you. Do not drop the rod until the line is straight out in front of you. This is the position of the line during the casting stoke. ***Note:*** *The rod tip and hand both travel in a straight plane during the cast.*
ALEJANDRO GOMEZ

On the forward stroke, make sure to accelerate the rod even more quickly than you would on your forehand cast. This will create more energy and make the flies move faster. Make an abrupt stop at two o'clock. This will make the flies return to you at a high rate of speed and dive straight down through the water column.
ALEJANDRO GOMEZ

THE ROLL CAST

Once you master the basic casting stroke, the next cast of importance to learn is the roll cast. This is a way to present your flies to fish when there are obstructions behind you. It's less about power and more about proper technique. The modern weight-forward fly lines that we use today generally have shorter and heavier front tapers, which are ideal for this type of casting.

When beginning the roll cast, stand upright with your shoulders up. You are in the ready position with the rod at your side, the same as for the basic cast. Slowly bring your rod alongside your body until you get to the ten o'clock position. If done properly, the line will be in a D-shape behind your rod. Accelerate the rod forward the same way you would when making the forward cast in your basic casting stroke (remember the sliding rail). When the rod gets to the two o'clock position, come to a complete stop.

If done properly, what you will see is that the loop behind you becomes a circle; the power that you transferred through the line will enable this circle to unravel and present your flies straight out in front of you. This cast also serves as a way to get line out of your rod to make a longer forward cast. When you're indicator-nymphing, it also enables you to make short casts more quickly than if you attempted a basic backcast.

You can see here that the line is brought back behind your position; remember to pause for a moment before your casting stroke. ALEJANDRO GOMEZ

Once the casting stroke is made, you can see the loop traveling down the line.
ALEJANDRO GOMEZ

As the loop gets farther away, it gets smaller due to the distance and decrease in power. ALEJANDRO GOMEZ

Finally, the line is laid out and the cast is made. ALEJANDRO GOMEZ

THE TUCK CAST

The last cast of major importance is called the tuck cast. You generally use this cast when you are fishing nymphs. It enables you to get your flies down to the bottom very quickly once they hit the water. When making a tuck cast, come forward as if you were making a forward cast, but at the end of your forward cast, abruptly stop the rod. Bring the rod back by bending your wrist and bringing your hand toward you, about two inches.

This is one of the few times that you will break your wrist when casting. Doing this little snap with your wrist and bringing your hand and the rod back will cause your flies to dart back at the end of the cast, toward your position. They will dive right into the water and begin sinking straight down. A normal cast will cause the flies to "hinge" down through the water column and be out of the target zone during less of the drift. The tuck cast achieves a greater depth, faster. This cast is extremely useful when you are employing the various subsurface or nymph-fishing techniques discussed in chapter 4.

In a tuck cast, the same forward cast is made as in the basic cast. However, the rod is abruptly stopped, which makes the fly accelerate at a high rate of speed. JUSTIN IDE

This is the end of the tuck cast. It is clear that the abrupt stopping of the rod has enabled the fly to dive into the water. The leader is already coming toward the author, which shows how the nymphs are going to enter the water column and achieve depth. JUSTIN IDE

CHAPTER 3

The Water Bodies

Whether you are standing in a mountain stream in Pennsylvania or a tailwater fishery in Montana, fly-fishing for trout means being in a serene place. Trout are delicate creatures by nature, requiring cold, clean water in order to survive. These days, that translates to some of the most beautiful places in the world. There are five main water bodies in which anglers pursue trout, and they're all extraordinary. They are small mountain or headwater streams, larger freestone streams or rivers, tailwaters, spring creeks, and lakes or reservoirs.

STREAMS AND TAILWATERS

Let's start with the smallest of the five fisheries. *Small mountain streams* provide excellent opportunities to catch wild trout throughout the United States. Due to the fact that these are generally the headwaters of larger rivers, stocking generally does not occur at a high rate. This is one reason why many indigenous species in the United States still have intact populations in these small fluvial systems. On a recent trip to Vermont, fishing a tributary to the Otter River, I found rainbows established in the lower sections, but the farther up I went, the more rainbow numbers declined and native brookies increased.

This is a low gradient riffle, which are typically found on tail water fisheries throughout the country. AARON JASPER

Small mountain streams offer some unique opportunities. Blind-casting dry flies is often the most successful way to tease trout from their holding lies. Once, in Yellowstone Park, I saw the tail of a cutthroat trout behind a rock. I crept close and cast my stimulator in front of the rock. That trout came out and took my fly with a vengeance. When fishing these types of streams and prospecting with the dry fly, it is extremely important to cast your flies everywhere possible. You never know where the trout are going to be holding. The water temperatures are generally very cold, meaning the trout can be nearly anywhere. The best time to fish these streams is when they are low. Another thing to keep in mind is that the trout in these streams do not have a very long season to feed. They do most of their feeding during the summer months. Headwater streams generally do not have the same diversity of insects that the lower reaches of these rivers have, making the trout more opportunistic.

Freestone streams are very special, formed when many headwater streams come together to create a larger, undammed river. Their biodiversity is amazing, with varied and prolific insect hatches. Some examples of freestone streams with prolific insect activity would be the Yellowstone and Big Hole Rivers in Montana, Pine Creek and Penns Creek in Pennsylvania, and the Housatonic River in Connecticut. These are all fly-fishing meccas.

Freestone streams are extremely fertile. Plant matter, such as fallen leaves during autumn, get washed into these larger rivers, providing food for many macroinvertebrates. Additionally, silt gets washed into these rivers from the tributaries, creating habitat for insect species that burrow in the silt. This silt is also full of nutrients due to the fact that plant matter is deposited throughout. Weed growth on the banks also provides habitat for many invertebrate species, as well as prey, such as minnows that larger trout feed on. Because of all these factors, some of the largest trout caught by fly rod are caught on larger freestone river systems.

Tailwater fisheries present unique opportunities for fly fishers. These are man-made fisheries that are the result of damming up the river systems for flood control, irrigation, hydroelectric power, or drinking water. The water below these dams generally flows at a constant rate, with the exception of streams below dams where power is generated and during times of flooding or irrigation. Tailwater river systems can range from infertile midge fisheries, as with the San Juan River in New Mexico, to extremely fertile rivers like the West Branch of the Delaware in New York. The fertility of tailwater streams depends greatly upon the reservoir "turning over." When a reservoir turns over, the nutrients which were deposited in the reservoir bottom are redistributed throughout the water column in the reservoir. As water drains from the reservoir, passes through the dam, and continues down the river, the nutrients are redeposited throughout the river system. This depositing of nutrients generally takes place more frequently in reservoirs that are drawn down to lower levels, typically the case in those that were created for flood control and drinking water purposes.

Driftboats are sort of the golf carts of fly fishing, taking you from hole to hole and allowing you to fish the river comfortably. They are very helpful on larger rivers.
AARON JASPER

Tailwater fisheries such as the White River in Arkansas and the Big Horn River in Montana follow an entirely different set of rules. Both of these fisheries have excellent weed growth, which provides habitat for the invertebrate species that are found in these waterways. The most common available food sources in these tailwaters are midges, freshwater shrimp, and cress bugs. Other available food sources in larger tailwaters are generally not as diverse as those found in tailwaters created by shallower impoundments. Generally you will have a few species of caddis. Out west you will see that the tailwaters have hatches of small stoneflies called yellow sallies. Mayfly species are often limited to sulfurs, pale morning duns (PMDs), and blue-winged olives of various sizes.

On tailwater fisheries, which begin as outflows from the bottom of deeper lakes, you will often find similar insect biomass that you would find on larger freestone streams. This is because of the nutrient cycling

Due to the consistently good fishing conditions, tailwater trout fisheries receive a great deal of pressure. Here is a lineup of boats on Montana's Beaverhead River.
AARON JASPER

that goes on within the lake, leading to more nutrient-rich water coming out from the bottom of the dam. (Top-draw dams are an obvious exception to this generalization.)

The majority of the tailwaters in the East benefit from the higher biomass of a shallower lake. The Lehigh River in Pennsylvania is a prominent example. Other similar tailwaters are the West Branch of the Delaware in New York, the Farmington River in Connecticut, and the Savage River in Maryland. All of these streams come from shallower impoundments, which allow for greater nutrient cycling.

Tailwater fisheries are responsible for some of the largest trout ever caught. The White and North Fork Rivers in Arkansas are responsible for multiple trout over thirty pounds. Due to the more-stable nature of these types of fisheries, the average-size trout is generally greater than what we see in freestone streams. This is one of the main draws of tailwater fisheries: They provide consistently good conditions and larger fish.

Tailwater fisheries are often an oasis for trout in an area that normally would not support them. Large impoundments offer a "thermal bank" of cold water that can be drawn on all season long, when normally the water would become too warm to sustain trout. Many great trout fisheries in the United States only exist because of this consistent temperature. Great fisheries like the San Juan River in New Mexico or the White River system of Arkansas and Missouri would be completely inhospitable to trout in the high heat of summer.

Conversely, these same "thermal bank" impoundments offer consistent temperatures in the cold of winter. Fisheries such as the West Branch of the Delaware or the Farmington in Connecticut fish very well in the deep of winter.

SPRING CREEKS

Generally found in valleys, *spring creeks* usually have low gradients and a very constant flow. They are typically affected very little by snowmelt

Montana's DePuy Spring Creek HEATH POTTER

and rain events. Welling up from an aquifer through limestone or other porous rock, water comes to the surface, consistently cold and clear, regardless of the season. Limestone creeks also have a consistent pH, which can lead to very high plant growth and associated invertebrate habitat. Trout in spring creeks, because of the consistent flow, are generally very aware of their surroundings, making them spooky by nature.

Clear water provides great visibility, both to you and the trout. Walking up to a spring creek, the angler needs to take a very careful approach. Chances are if you've seen a fish in a spring creek, he's seen you too. Much like some tailwaters, spring creeks tend to be very fertile, even if they do not typically have a diverse biomass. The main species of invertebrates that trout prey upon are midges, freshwater shrimp, cress bugs, sulfurs, PMDs, and various blue-winged olive species. What this means to fly anglers is that these trout are particularly discerning when it comes to imitations of these insects.

Sneaking a look at likely water can pay off big-time when fishing to wary spring creek trout. HEATH POTTER

The author lands a nice wild brown trout at DuPuy Spring Creek near Livingston, Montana. HEATH POTTER

Spring creeks are fishable nearly 365 days a year. Angler pressure is consistently high, meaning that trout are generally more selective. Some of the most famous spring creeks in the country are found in Pennsylvania.

The Letort, Falling Spring Branch, and Big Spring Creek are three of the most famous limestone streams in Pennsylvania. All three have very storied histories. Additionally, the spring creeks in Paradise Valley near Livingston, Montana, are some of the very best in the world. Silver Creek in Sun Valley, Idaho, might be one of the most famous spring creeks in the world. In addition, the Harriman Ranch on the Henry's Fork in Idaho fishes much like a spring creek. Spring creeks can be fulfilling to fish but also very frustrating, offering probably some of the most challenging water in all of fly fishing.

STILL WATER

Lakes and reservoirs are often overlooked as fly-fishing destinations, even though there are abundant trout populations in the majority of lakes and reservoirs throughout the West. And while there is some stocking that goes on, the majority of these fish are wild. If you go to some of the higher-elevation lakes, you'll catch indigenous species of cutthroat in the West and brook trout in the East.

Fishing for trout in Western still water is much more popular than in the East. This is due mainly to the fact that the trout feed on insects. In the East the majority of the lakes are stocked with smallish trout that are primarily meant to create put-and-take fisheries. Additionally, the reservoirs in the East, which can contain trout in excess of twenty pounds, feed on alewives or herring. This makes it very difficult for fly anglers to catch them. It is hard to imitate a large baitfish like a herring in a lake where the water is not moving.

Fly anglers in the East can enjoy a brief window for fishing to mostly stocked trout in lakes. The warmer summer months in the East generally push the trout to great depths. These lakes form what's called a *thermocline.* This is where the sun's light penetrates the water, causing the upper layer to warm up to temperatures that are unsafe for trout. Because the sun's light can't penetrate all the way to the bottom of most lakes, there is a cold layer of water beneath this warmer layer. This is where the trout spend their summer months.

In the West, while you do have extremely warm daytime temperatures, the nighttime temperatures generally are much lower and thus create lower average water temperatures. This leads to the trout cruising in shallower water, meaning they are more easily targeted by fly fishers. Some of the best dry-fly fishing I've ever experienced has taken place on lakes. The Callibaetis hatch on most Western lakes is a spectacle that needs to be experienced by every fly angler. If someone travels to the West and is not fishing still water, he is simply cheating himself.

THREE TROUT LIES

Trout in running water, whether small streams, freestone rivers, tail-waters, or spring creeks, choose to live where their basic needs are met. A *lie* is a fly-fishing term for where a trout chooses to hold in a stream. A trout's three purposes in life are to avoid predation, eat, and reproduce. Trout can be found in areas that meet all three of these requirements: holding lies, safety lies, and prime lies. A *holding lie* is an area where the trout can both feed and find some degree of safety from predators. A *safety lie* is where a trout goes when spooked by either an angler or a predator. A *prime lie* offers a place where a trout can hide from predators and feed opportunistically. These types of lies are generally found where you have in-stream structure, such as large boulders or undercut banks.

Learning about these lies and knowing where to find them in various water types can mean the difference between a great day and a bad day on the water. Looking at the water and reading the signs and clues about these lies will help you to target your fish and determine the method you use to catch them.

CHAPTER 4

Nymphing

All species of trout, regardless of size, spend the vast majority of their lives feeding on nymphs. Many of us have heard the adage that trout eat 90 percent of their diet subsurface. The real percentage is actually higher. And while dry-fly purists may look down on nymphing, the

The author is looking over a very productive section of pocket water for likely holding ties before beginning his fishing. Looking and observing the water can yield increases in catch rates. By stopping and looking you will be able to take in more than you would if you were to simply step in and start nymphing. JUSTIN IDE

Danny Marino, ex-captain of the USA Youth Fly Fishing Team, nymphs a productive riffle on the Housatonic River in Connecticut. SAM MARINO

truth is that nymphing is one of the most difficult forms of fly fishing to master. Once an angler becomes proficient at it, however, it becomes possible to catch trout on a more-consistent basis.

Nymphing forces anglers to learn how to read the water and make approximations of where they think the fish are holding. It is not like dry-fly fishing, where you see the fish rise. When trout are rising they give up their location, and it's all about making the proper presentation. When fishing subsurface with nymphs, you have to "hunt" the fish down and figure out where they are holding. Although my first trout was caught on a dry fly, I am a nymph fisherman at heart. I enjoy the three-dimensional challenges presented by nymphing.

There are several methods of nymphing, and each has a certain water type in which it is productive. Learning the following three methods of nymphing will enable you to approach many different water types and have consistent success. The three techniques of nymphing most widely used by fly anglers are tight-line (or high-stick) nymphing, indicator nymphing, and European nymphing. The latter has grown in popularity in recent years due to its effectiveness.

The majority of trout over twenty inches that are caught each year are taken on nymphs. Even though larger trout, especially browns, become predators, they never forget that insects were a part of their diet and will feed on them, especially during heavy insect activity. Many anglers think that streamer fishing is the best way to catch the largest trout. However, keep in mind that large trout do not like leaving the comfort of their surroundings. When a large trout is in a riffle feeding on nymphs, you are more likely to catch it due to the fact that it's comfortable in its lie and is feeding. When fishing other techniques, you're relying heavily on the trout coming out of its comfort zone to take your offering.

TIGHT-LINE OR HIGH-STICK NYMPHING

High-stick nymphing was pioneered by Joe Brooks, George Harvey, and Joe Humphreys in the early years of American nymph fishing. Before George Harvey, few anglers fished subsurface, and if they did, it was

The author tight-line-nymphs a smaller stream. This technique works extremely well on smaller streams, where you can get close to the fish. BRYAN HAYWOOD

with wet flies. George Harvey was a true innovator and experimented with split shot as well as underwater nymphs. He was likely inspired by nymph fishermen from Europe. Many old-time fly anglers (cattle barons) from Wyoming were taught to high-stick by visiting Italian and English fly fishers as long ago as the late 1800s.

Tackle

High-stick nymphing generally requires a nine- to ten-foot rod and a line between a 4- and a 5-weight. Joe Humphreys liked to use a fine-diameter running line due to the short distances generally cast. Right now, fly lines like RIO Trout LT are the state of the art for this method. It allows for good control, a fine touch, and connection to the flies.

Water Types

This technique is deadly when you are in close proximity to the trout. During high-water events, for instance, the more turbulent, off-color

Here the author lands a trout he took using a tandem of midges, with split shot added in order to get the flies down. Note the shallow water at the head of the pool.
HEATH POTTER

This two-foot brown trout was caught by the author on a small stream using split shot and tight-line nymphing techniques. HEATH POTTER

water enables you to get closer to the fish. Trout can see at some very amazing distances during periods when the water is clear, but when the water visibility is decreased, they are not able to discern the flies as readily. A trout that can see six feet when the water is low and clear can only see eighteen inches when the water is high and off-color. Use this to your advantage!

During periods of high water, trout often get pushed out of their usual holding lies. This can be due to both increased water volume and lower visibility. The average trout does not feel comfortable with the decreased visibility caused by silt and suspended matter in the water column. As a result, the trout will move to shallower water where there is sufficient light penetration, enabling it to see. When the water first comes up and is extremely muddy, trout will hold in as little as four to six inches of water. As the water starts to clear, the trout will begin to make their way back toward the middle of the stream. It is important to remember that both a decreased water volume and an increase in visibility need to occur for the trout to return to their usual holding lies.

When the water rises—for instance, after a rain or a release from a dam—the smaller trout are the first to be pushed to slower areas, generally found on the margins of the stream. Often, the larger fish will be caught off guard as they shift to a new position in the stream. This is why you see a disproportionate number of large trout being caught during high water.

Fishing areas where the trout can be pushed during high water are the key to success. You can eliminate up to 90 percent of the total water in a stream during high water. You want to focus your casts in areas where the water is deflected by structure, such as downed trees or islands. Trout will often be found holding directly behind them. Back eddies, where the current runs upstream, are also great holding locations. These are generally formed as streams rise and the water is dispersed from the streambed. These types of structures create small holding lies where the fish can seek refuge from the fast, turbulent water. Trout can also be found in surprisingly high numbers on the inside bends of a turn in a stream.

This trout fell for a Juju Baetis fished on a tight-line presentation. TOM WALSH

A few years ago, I was guiding a great deal on the Housatonic River in northwest Connecticut. This is a large freestone stream which is susceptible to high runoff, both from snowmelt as well as rain. The river had run extremely high for a long period, and I was finding success when other guides were having a tough go of it. I knew of a half-dozen good spots and would fish them thoroughly. One of these spots was only about the size of a minivan, but we took more eighteen-inch browns from this location than any other section of the stream. Why? The water was so high that all of the fish from that mile of stream had been pushed into this one small area.

Another reason to nymph with the high-stick method is what I call the *cased caddis phenomenon.* Cased caddis are filter feeders, found in nearly every stream that also holds trout. During periods of high water they get washed off rocks and are extremely vulnerable. This is especially true in river systems that are affected by heavy runoff due to snowmelt. Cased caddis also get washed off rocks when the water is high, making them an important food item for trout. I have watched trout that are holding in high water actively dislodging cased caddis with their tails before swimming downstream to feed on them.

When I was younger we used to keep some trout for the table. I always noticed that there were numerous bits and pieces of sand and plant matter in their stomachs. It took me a long time to figure out why. These were bits and pieces of cased caddis.

High-sticking also works extremely well in shallow water where you need to fish small flies with very little weight. You can achieve a very natural drift, even with the smallest of flies. This is especially true in river systems where trout feed on tiny midges and freshwater crustaceans in shallow water. This is exactly the type of water in which Joe Humphreys fishes. Central Pennsylvania is full of shallow streams where the most abundant food sources are midges and freshwater crustaceans. Even though I have learned many other techniques, I still find myself high-sticking when the situation arises.

Rigging Up

When fishing a tight-line/high-stick system, I use a nearly identical setup to the one I use for Czech/Polish nymphing (one branch of European nymphing; see the Czech/Polish nymphing section for a clearer explanation). Come off of the fly line with three feet of .019-inch stiff

TIGHT LINE NYMPHING

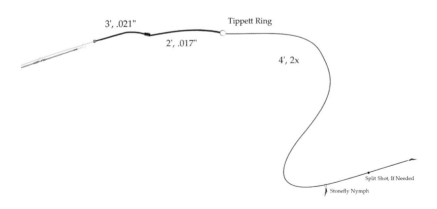

monofilament. Blood-knot a piece of .015-inch stiff monofilament to it. I like to use clear line for the butt section of my leader. Off of the butt section, attach a foot-long piece of fluorescent monofilament. The color can vary from fluorescent yellow to fluorescent orange. This will give you something to help detect strikes.

Off of the indicator section, attach your tippet. Fluoroflex Plus in 4X and 5X are common sizes for fishing in high water. Attach four feet of tippet to the end of the indicator. Surgeon-knot another piece of tippet of the same diameter to the existing section. Attach one nymph to the dropper tag and the second nymph to the remaining tag end. Make sure that the nymphs are about twenty inches apart; this will result in less tangling of the flies. The debate is ongoing about whether fluorocarbon tippet is worth it, but for strength and abrasion resistance, it can't be beat. When fishing the tight line technique, it's important not to use flies that are weighted. Using flies with brass and glass beads are acceptable. The weight used to make the flies achieve depth is the split shot and having weighted flies will cause the flies to hang up on the bottom of the stream. Using unweighted flies enable the flies to stay off the bottom and in view of the fish.

The weighting of your leader is where things get complicated. Here's a little insight: For deeper, faster water, place your split shot about twenty inches above the first fly. You might have to vary your weight depending on velocity and speed of the current. When fishing in shallower water zones, place a small amount of weight above your first fly, and then place a lesser amount of weight between your two flies. This will enable them to ride parallel to the bottom of the stream without getting hung up. For split shot I like to use green-colored tin shot. I think that in heavily pressured streams, trout get used to seeing bright silver split shot and will spook; green, camouflage split shot gives you an advantage.

The Cast

The cast for the short leader is very simple. It starts off with water tension. Keep your elbow bent at a 90-degree angle. Pick a target on the opposite bank that is approximately 45 degrees up and across from your position. Using the water tension to cast the nymphs, simply straighten your arm out. Doing this and following through at your target will enable the nymphs to be cast out at your target. After the cast, keep the rod tip up. Once the rod tip is up, simply keep it ahead of your flies as they drift downstream. This will enable you to keep contact with your flies, which is essential to strike detection. Once the flies reach a 45-degree position below you, make a quick wrist flick to get your nymphs back out of the water. Repeat this sequence for each cast. The mechanics of the cast are quite easy to learn.

INDICATOR NYMPHING

You can see here that the author is indicator-nymphing deeper water by both the style of indicator and the depth of the water in which he is wading. This trout decided to put on an aerial display. ALEJANDRO GOMEZ

Introduction

The beauty of nymph fishing is that it's a constantly changing puzzle; no one method can cover every situation.

I grew up fly-fishing smaller streams with my grandfather. We fished tight-line, Joe Humphreys–style nymphing setups, with no indicators.

This was very effective until I started fishing larger rivers and streams, where presenting my flies at a distance was necessary. One particular day comes to mind: I stepped out at a large riffle on the West Branch of the Delaware. The riffle was wide, and shallower than I was used to, and the trout were more spread out. It was not the usual pocket water that we often fished together. I spent some fruitless time on that water before deciding to take a trip up to the West Branch Angler. I bought a package of indicators, thinking they might be just what I needed to present my flies at a distance. I was right; with a very crude setup, I was able to catch numerous wild trout, where just a few hours ago the only thing I was doing was getting some casting practice.

Water Types to Fish Indicator-Style

Certain water types are ideal for fishing indicators. The method comes into its own, for instance, when you have a riffle with a very slow gradient change. These are the types of riffled water that you often find on tailwater streams—large expanses of water where the river goes from a very shallow depth to a deeper one over a great amount of distance.

When fishing a shallow, low-gradient riffle, long casts up and across are often needed to present your nymphs without spooking the fish. ALEJANDRO GOMEZ

Here, the author makes an upstream mend, useful when the surface currents start to pull on the indicator. A mend is simply made by picking up the rod and repositioning the line to compensate for the variances in current. ALEJANDRO GOMEZ

In areas like this it is very important to keep your flies in the water for a long period of time. In these low-gradient riffles, the trout are often spread apart over a great area, and the need for longer, drag-free drifts is of upmost importance to the angler. Using a strike indicator and making long casts to varying degrees upstream will enable you to cover lots of water throughout the day.

Indicator nymphing is also great on runs with a constant depth. With little depth change, the angler is able to set up a leader that allows him or her to maintain contact with the flies throughout the entire run. You are able to judge the proper amount of weight and distance needed between the indicator and the weights.

The third scenario where indicator nymphing comes into its own is in fishing ledges. Being able to rig up your leader in anticipation of the depth "after" the depth change is essential; other nymphing methods do not allow you to do this as easily.

The author has hooked up to a nice trout using a deepwater strike indicator setup. Notice that he is up to his waist in the stream; this means that the water he is fishing is as deep as, or deeper than, where he is standing. JUSTIN IDE

I would not recommend indicator-nymphing in water where there is a great deal of depth change. In water commonly referred to as *pocket water*, it often becomes too difficult to make the weight changes necessary to maintain contact with your fly and thus see, or feel, your strikes. Another detriment to indicator nymphing in areas where there is a lot of depth change is that you run the risk of becoming snagged on the bottom due to your inability to control the depth of your flies throughout the drift.

The Leader

A good nymphing leader should taper quickly from a heavy butt section to a lighter end. It should be roughly half butt section and half tippet. Using lighter leader after the butt section decreases tippet drag and allows you to get your flies down with the least amount of weight possible. This is beneficial to detecting strikes.

Leader Construction

To build a leader for indicator nymphing, I start by attaching, directly off my fly line, a two-foot section of .021-inch red Amnesia. To this I attach a three-foot piece of brown Maxima, or any stiff .012-inch mono-filament. This will be the piece that holds the indicator. To tie these first and second pieces of the butt section together, use a blood knot. The butt section should be, in total, five feet in length.

After attaching the butt section, tie on a small tippet ring. This will make changing the leader sections easier and will decrease the num-ber of difficult knots that you will eventually have to tie. Next, tie on a five-foot section of 4X Fluoroflex Plus. To this section attach another small tippet ring. I place my weights above the tippet ring, avoiding the common problem of split shot sliding down the line toward the flies. Next, tie a twenty-inch piece of 5X to 6X fluorocarbon to the tippet ring. Choose the diameter of the fluorocarbon based upon water clarity (5X for dirty, 6X for clear water).

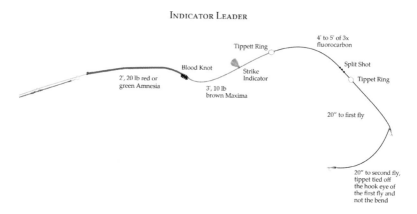

INDICATOR LEADER

When indicator-nymphing, use two flies. Tie on another twenty-inch piece of fluorocarbon to the hook eye of the first nymph. Make sure it's at least twenty inches. If the distance between your nymphs is too short, there's a greater risk of the trout getting foul-hooked on the second fly. I prefer the hook eye to the bend in the hook.

Fly Selection

Since you are using split shot as your primary weight, it is important not to use weighted nymphs. Using weighted nymphs will not only make you more vulnerable to snags but will also keep your offerings below the fish and thus out of their view. Remember, trout have eyes on top of their heads and either look forward or up to take food. Using brass beads as an attractor on the larger nymph is often a good idea, especially in higher water, but tungsten is simply too heavy for this style of fishing. The smaller nymphs can have a bead made of tungsten or brass. This is because the mass of the fly is not heavy enough to drag along the bottom, due to the water deflection on the streambed.

Indicators (Trapped-Air vs. Yarn)

Each indicator has its proper time and place. I really like trapped-air indicators such as Fish Pimp and Thingamabobbers when you are fishing in close range. They float heavy amounts of weight but do not

This large tailwater brown trout was taken on a size 20 WD-40 nymph at the conclusion of a Hendrickson hatch, right at the beginning of the behavioral drift cycle.
ANTHONY MACCHIAROLA

protrude far enough from the water's surface to be seen from long distances. Larger, more-visible indicators also tend to compromise your ability to detect a strike; it takes more force from the fish to sink the indicator.

Yarn indicators are best for fishing at great distances, mainly due to the fact that the fibers of the yarn protrude from the surface of the stream and are easily seen at great distances. The one drawback with yarn indicators is that you should pretreat them before use with a heavy silicone, like LOON payette. After applying the paste, simply brush it out and you will have an indicator that is fluffy and easy to see at great distances. These indicators are inexpensive and readily available and can be modified on the stream for optimal performance. Some people also say they present a more-natural appearance and are less likely to spook fish.

Weight Choices

For indicator nymphing, I like to use tin split shot rather than lead. I used to be a huge lead fan, but Torrey Collins, manager of Housatonic River Outfitters in Connecticut, showed me that there is not much difference in the size and mass of tin versus lead and that tin is a much harder metal than lead, meaning it bounces off rocks rather than snagging in cracks. When Torrey claimed to lose 25 percent fewer perfect flies using a less-toxic material, I thought he was joking. But now I know that, if anything, he was understating; it might be more like half. Additionally, the shot without the tabs for removal tends to also snag less.

When choosing split shot I usually like to use one of four sizes: AB, BB, 1, or 4; 4 is best for very shallow, low-gradient, riffled water up to about two feet deep. Size 1 works well for water up to three feet deep, with a moderate current. For higher-water situations, use AB and BB. Remember, you don't have to limit yourself to only one split shot; it might take multiple split shot to get your flies down.

If using multiple split shot, try to avoid placing them in the same place on the line above the micro ring. Putting even a few millimeters between your split shot on the line will enable you to avoid becoming snagged in the crevices of rocks, ultimately losing flies. The more area the weight covers as it drifts across the bottom of the stream, the less likely it is to get snagged.

Where to Position the Indicator

As previously mentioned, the indicator goes on the butt section, where the diameter of line is .012 inch. When adjusting the indicator on the line, make the distance between the indicator and the weight one-half to two times the water depth. This depends on the speed of the current. The faster the current, the longer the distance should be between the indicator and the split shot. Many anglers mistakenly believe that the distance between the flies and the indicator is the most important thing, but when you are indicator-nymphing, the indicator location in relation to the weight is the most important factor to consider in getting your flies successfully to the bottom. The split shot are the means by which

Small flies catch nice fish. Here is a nice rainbow trout taken in some heavy current on a size 20 WD-40 nymph. JUSTIN IDE

47

the flies achieve depth. What occurs beyond the split shot, with the exception of fly selection, has little to do with the fish taking the flies.

By setting up your indicator for one-half to twice the water depth, you allow your nymphs to be presented at the same current speed as that found on the bottom of the stream. You will notice your indictor slow down, so you will be tighter to your flies, which will in turn increase your strike detection. Often you will notice the bubbles and surface currents of the stream passing your indicator as your flies are drifting downstream. Remember, if the indicator is moving at the same speed as the surface of the stream, it's moving too fast! It should always move slightly slower than the surface. The indicator needs to reflect the speed of the *bottom* of the stream, not the surface.

Methods of Presentation

There are two ways to present nymphs fished with a strike indicator, and both involve making an upstream cast. With the first method, you fish the indicator directly upstream of your position and retrieve the flies as they

Here you see the author setting the hook on a trout that took his nymphs below his position. Notice that he set the hook behind his position with the current. Do not set the hook upstream across your body when the flies are below you; this will make for slack in your line, possibly resulting in lost fish. ALEJANDRO GOMEZ

drift toward you. This is the easiest, because it involves the least amount of mending to get your flies to the bottom. The presentation is simple: Make an upstream cast. As the indicator drifts back toward your position, strip in line at a rate that matches the indicator coming toward you.

The second and more-productive method involves casting the flies upstream at a 45-degree angle. Once the flies are presented, you have to mend the line in accordance with the direction of the current. This allows your flies to achieve full depth. By "mending" the line, I mean picking up a section of the line with the rod and positioning it counter to the surface currents. When there is a faster surface current between you and the indicator, it is important to mend the line upstream. This will keep the indicator in position, therefore allowing the flies to sink properly. When the current is slower between you and the indicator, you need to mend the fly line downstream.

Here you can clearly see how the author picks up the rod and lifts the line to put it behind the indicator, achieving a dead-drift presentation. This allows the flies to drift naturally with the current. ALEJANDRO GOMEZ

Here the author performs a stack mend. Much like a roll cast toward the strike indicator, a stack mend puts slack into the line and keeps the indicator moving freely, which allows the flies to sink more effectively. ALEJANDRO GOMEZ

When making this presentation, think about a bowl. When the cast is made, the flies and split shot are at the top of the bowl. When the mend is made, the flies sink and go straight to the bottom of the bowl. At the end of the drift, the flies come back up to the surface (tip of the bowl) and then are presented again to the fish.

One last thing that you can do, which can be especially productive in low-gradient riffles, is to feed some line out right after the mend. This will allow you to keep your flies in the water longer, therefore giving more fish the possibility of seeing them.

Once the indicator drops, set the hook. Anytime the indicator moves irregularly during the drift, assume a fish is taking your flies. You'll often be hitting bottom, but the more often you set the hook, the more you will realize that irregular movement in the indicator is actually a trout hitting your nymphs. Don't hesitate to try to set the hook.

Here you can see that the author rotates his hips as the indicator drifts downstream. It is important to follow or track your indicator downstream as you wait for a reason to set the hook. ALEJANDRO GOMEZ

And speaking of setting the hook: Try to set the hook with the current. Never lift the rod across your body, up-current. The hook set should be a sweeping downstream motion where your arm and body work together to create enough force to both take up slack in the line and drive the hook point into the trout's jaw. A friend of mine introduced me to the concept of setting the hook downstream, and it has made a huge increase in my hookup to landing rates. When the drift is downstream of your position, the hook set should be across your body and toward your back shoulder.

Tackle for Indicator Nymphing

For indicator nymphing, a fast-action, ten-foot, four- or five-weight rod is ideal. There are even times when a ten-foot, six-weight is appropriate, especially when there is a great deal of wind or when you are using larger flies and heavier weights on larger rivers. In bigger water, a fast-action rod is an excellent choice because of its ability to recover, or straighten out, after making a cast or manipulating the line. Effective mending and line control are always necessary components of indicator nymphing. You can even use a longer switch-style, four- to five-weight rod in larger rivers in order to make longer, more-effective drifts. This is especially true on many of the larger Eastern and Western tailwaters. Many companies make specialized nymphing lines, such as the RIO Indicator line. These lines have a long, heavy, front taper, which helps in the casting and mending of indicator rigs.

EUROPEAN NYMPHING METHODS

European-style nymphing techniques have rapidly become quite popular here in the United States. Many European countries have rules that disallow extra weight, like split shot, during nymphing. All of the weight must be incorporated into the design of the fly. In addition, many countries do not allow floating strike indicators.

Some anglers see these European nymphing techniques as nothing more than tight-line nymphing, but whatever you call them, after trying these techniques out on your home streams, you won't look back. Nymph fishing will never be the same.

History

European nymphing was invented primarily as a way to fish high-gradient freestone streams in Eastern Europe. These areas are home to large populations of grayling and brown trout. Grayling are accustomed to a human presence and often shoal up in large numbers in the riffles and pockets that abound in these streams. Europeans needed a technique that would allow them to access these areas. European nymphing is characterized by the use of a short line, which allows the angler to detect more strikes and increase catch rate. As soon as the fish hits the flies, the angler can feel the energy travel through the short line, and he can see the line move as well. This technique works equally well for both seasoned experts and beginners.

Czech/Polish Nymphing

Former world fly-fishing champion Vladi Trzebunia could be credited with popularizing and introducing Czech/Polish nymphing styles to America. Vladi was one of the Team USA coaches and taught anglers like Pete Erickson, Jeff Currier, Jay Buchner, and Norman Maktima how to Czech/Polish-nymph on his home rivers of Poland. He visited the United States often to teach the style.

My first experience with Czech nymphing was on the South Branch of the Raritan River, my home stream. After many conversations with Davy Wotton, a world-renowned fly fisherman, regarding this new technique, I was ready to try my hand. Armed with a wide array of the required weighted flies, I headed to the stream. It was a crisp March morning, and the South Branch had fished well all winter. There were many holdover fish, as well as about two thousand recently stocked brook trout—all good signs. I started off fishing a large cased caddis pattern as an anchor fly and a pink caddis larva and natural olive caddis as the droppers.

The author fishes in a section of stream with a very high gradient. Czech nymphing excels in this type of water. JUSTIN IDE

53

I started the morning fishing behind a gentleman whom I watched catch a few fish in a popular spot. After he left the spot, I stepped into the water and cast out my flies. To my surprise, I was into fish before he'd even left the area. I released my first fish and, on my next cast, was into another. This continued throughout the day. I caught many fish, some coming from places that I had never tried to fish before because the spots were not conducive to indicator fishing, which was my primary means of fishing before this day.

I rarely fish indicators now unless I am on a low-gradient stream. Though the Czech technique took some time to learn, it is one of the most productive means of nymph fishing I have ever come across, especially when fishing nymphs close. After fishing many of the same spots that I have fished with indicators, I'm finding myself catching twice as many fish, including some truly large ones.

Presentation

The presentation of flies in Czech nymphing is similar to many other short-line nymphing techniques, such as the Humphreys method,

The author casts heavily weighted nymphs in heavy pocket water using a Czech/Polish style of nymphing. JUSTIN IDE

where the nymphs are fished on a tight line. There are, however, some distinguishing characteristics of Czech nymphing. The primary difference is that the flies are weighted, and there is no additional weight (like split shot) added to the line. The weight is incorporated into the design of the fly, therefore enabling the flies to get to the bottom. Additionally, the leader design, unlike conventional methods of nymphing, is very simple, often containing three sections or less.

The method of presentation is quite simple. The angle of the cast is anywhere from 20 to 40 degrees up and slightly across-stream. In addition to keeping a high rod angle, make sure that the rod stays slightly ahead of the flies. The line should have a slight arc and not be tight to the flies. If the line is tight to the flies, it means that the flies are too heavy for the run, and lighter flies should be substituted. The flies may drift slightly below your position in the stream, although not more than five or ten feet, as this method is intended for fishing short drifts.

Czech/Polish-style nymphing originated as a style of nymphing used to catch grayling in Europe. CHRISTOPHE LEDUC

The short drifts allow for better coverage because the angler is "gridding" out the stream, letting many of the casts overlap. When the casts are overlapping, the flies are presented to the same fish in varying manners and at different angles. Some trout will take the flies as they are descending into the water; others will take them mid-drift; and still others will take them at the end of the drift. For this reason, the end of your drift should never be neglected.

As the flies drift past, begin to lower your rod tip. At the end of the drift give a slight hook set. This does two things: First, the gentle lift might represent an insect emerging on the surface of the stream. Second, the trout might be drifting backwards with the flies; this sudden hook set enables you to catch fish where takes are almost undetectable, based on how the fish takes the flies and moves with them. Hooking fish at the end of the drift is like finding a ten-dollar bill in the pocket of your jeans before doing the wash.

Equipment

The equipment best suited for Czech nymphing is a medium-action rod from nine to eleven feet long. The rod should be full-flex and not tip-flex, as the full-flex rods are more sensitive to takes. Due to the tight-line style of Czech nymphing, the rod must be flexible enough to absorb the shock of a sudden take. Because strike detection is almost immediate, the natural response to set the hook might be too forceful; the more-flexible rod will enable you to protect your tippets.

The line weight of the rod is not as critical as one would think. The tuck cast used for Czech nymphing doesn't rely on false-casting, so rods designed for a 3- to 5-weight line are more than adequate. My preference is for a ten-foot, three- or four-weight rod. There are even times when I will use an eleven-foot rod. The equipment will be somewhat dictated by the size of the river. The longer rod will enable a greater reach and will aid in fishing tricky currents, which are often encountered in the pocket water where these techniques work best.

The author is about to release a nice wild brown trout caught while Czech-style nymphing in a stretch of heavy pocket water. JUSTIN IDE

Rigging

The leader setup for the Czech method is relatively simple: The entire leader system utilizes only three materials. For the butt section, I use three feet of twenty-pound Golden Stren, attaching it to my fly line using a three-turn clinch knot. Next, I knot two feet of fourteen-pound Golden Stren using a three-turn blood knot. My butt section is a total of five feet in length. The color in this section aids in detecting strikes. For these two pieces, you can also substitute fifteen- and twenty-pound-test Sunset Amnesia.

CZECH LURE

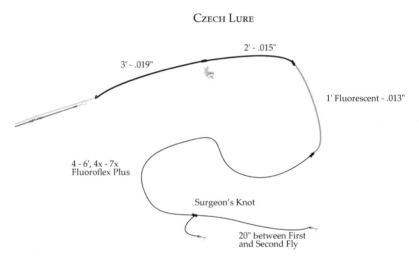

2' - .015"

3' - .019"

1' Fluorescent - .013"

4 - 6', 4x - 7x
Fluoroflex Plus

Surgeon's Knot

20" between First
and Second Fly

For my tippet, I generally use 5X fluorocarbon. The thin diameter aids in getting my flies down. There's less drag, as the tippet drops through the surface tension of the water. The entire leader is relatively short, usually twelve feet or less.

Water clarity and the types of flies being presented dictate the diameter of my tippet. For larger flies, which are generally used in heavy, fast water, I like to use 4X and 5X, depending on water clarity, but I generally prefer 5X. While this tippet might be a small diameter, it is surprisingly strong. All of the major premium brands of fluorocarbon are usually labeled well below their actual breaking strength. The 4X tends to tangle less than 5X and 6X.

As the size of the flies decreases, the need to use lighter tippet increases. With a pair of size 18 flies, I often use 6X Fluoroflex Plus for the tippet. The smaller the flies, the lighter they will be weighted, thus increasing the need to lessen the effects of surface current. Many European anglers will go so far as to use 7X, although I feel that this is unnecessary for most trout fishing. Finally, the overall depth of the water you plan to fish dictates tippet length. As a general rule, the length of the tippet is twice the depth of the water that you are going to be fishing.

Attaching the Flies

When tying on flies, they must be tied onto droppers. After the initial piece of tippet is attached to the butt section, I tie my first dropper by taking another piece of tippet (about thirty inches in length) and tying it to the piece coming from the butt section. I typically use a surgeon's knot, but you can also use the Orvis tippet knot to create your dropper tags. After tying the knot, clip the top tag. Tying the fly to the top tag end could possibly cause the knot to fail when hooking a fish. This will be the piece of leader to which your top dropper gets tied. The top dropper is typically the fly that is weighted less. The tag end should be four to six inches in length to allow for fly changes and to ensure twenty inches between flies. Your heavier anchor fly is the point fly, which is the last fly in your setup.

When fishing nymphs European style, a rubber-legged stonefly nymph makes a great anchor fly. JUSTIN IDE

This trout was fooled by a hot-spot-style nymph with a fluorescent thread collar.
JUSTIN IDE

Recommended Flies

Traditional Czech nymphs are generally designed to imitate the caddis larvae found in high-gradient freestone streams in Eastern Europe. Although traditional Czech nymphs are deadly, they are not essential when employing the technique.

In the United States we have a wider variety of food bases for the trout to eat, making the caddis flies less essential. Our trout feed on caddisfly larvae, mayfly nymphs, stoneflies, and other microinvertebrates and, in some river systems, crustaceans.

Regardless of the food source you choose to imitate, weighted nymphs are the key to this technique. In a pinch, you can place split shot between your two nymphs in case your flies are too light; however, tying weighted nymphs is relatively simple. Take your favorite trout nymphs and turn them into weighted nymphs by adding lead underbodies and tungsten bead heads. I carry various stonefly patterns as well as my favorite midges, and mayfly and caddisfly larvae. I used to be of

In the author's caddis larvae collection, you can see that there are dozens of larvae from medium to large in various shades of green and tan. These nymphs are commonly found in streams that are well suited for European nymphing. JUSTIN IDE

the mind-set that you had to tie fly patterns that were particular to this technique, but the more experience I gain, the more I realize that fly selection is not of major importance, as long as the fly is suggestive of a natural food source. Generic patterns like the hare's ear, prince, and pheasant tails are all great flies for starters.

The heavier flies are termed *anchor flies* because they take your offerings through the water column and into the trout's view. Some choice anchor flies include the Vladi's Condom Worm, the rubber-legged stonefly, the large-cased caddis, as well as the John Barr's Cranefly. These often incorporate large tungsten beads, a heavy lead underbody, or sometimes both.

Lighter flies include the Firefly, 265 nymphs, and various Czech-style nymphs to represent caddis larvae and various midges. Keep in mind that some of these flies will become anchors when fished in shallow water. A heavy fly such as the rubber-legged stonefly will sink too

This water is perfect for European-style nymphing. The many pockets and current seams create numerous holding lies, which are easily fished with both short- and long-line techniques. JUSTIN IDE

fast and get hung up in shallow water, whereas a size 12 tungsten-bead pheasant tail might be just the correct amount of weight.

When fishing this method I commonly use the heavier fly (or the anchor) on the point and the lighter fly tied on the dropper. In place of a weighted nymph, I might opt to fish soft hackle patterns that closely imitate emerging insects. This is especially deadly when fishing during a hatch.

French and Spanish Nymphing: Presenting Nymphs on Long Leaders

As the author casts toward shore, the coiled-style indicator is in focus, showing how the indicator should look as it drifts downstream. JUSTIN IDE

Introduction

As fly anglers, we are always looking for the newest gear and techniques. We do this to increase our catch rates and our enjoyment of the sport. However, there are times when we need to take a step back and look at the techniques that have historically been successful.

Anglers in France and Spain invented nymphing techniques that have been used to catch trout for generations, all over Europe and North America. It has been said that the Fario strain of brown trout, which inhabit French and Spanish streams, are the toughest trout to catch on the planet. They live in narrow, high-gradient mountain streams where the water is gin-clear and the density of trout is typically very low.

I visited France a few years back and can attest firsthand that these techniques are necessary to catch these extremely wary trout. If these techniques are successful on these difficult-to-catch fish, they will surely outproduce other methods here in the United States.

The first day I spent learning this technique will live in my memory for years to come. I consider myself a very competent angler and frequently fish a stream in my home state with lots of pocket water and a few scattered pools. I often use the South Branch of the Raritan as a testing ground for new techniques. I usually fish this water using strike indicators, and more recently I've tried short-line Euro nymphing

Because European nymphing techniques allow you to fish a larger variety of water, you're more apt to come upon a prize fish lurking behind a rock. The author took this twenty-eight-inch wild brown trout out of a stream in his home state of New Jersey.
TOM WALSH

techniques. On one trip, however, I had my rod rigged up "French" style, with a very long leader and two weighted flies.

The first stretch of water often produces about a dozen fish. I positioned myself midstream and began fishing my nymphs to every single holding area, and even some spots that I didn't think could hold a fish. I remembered my good friend Davy Wotton telling me that the French are so good at this, all they do is count to three and set the hook. He wasn't kidding. I did just that, casting my flies behind boulders, counting to three, and lifting the rod. Lo and behold, there was a trout attached to my line almost every time. It took me five hours to cover a section of stream that usually only takes me about one hour to go through. More fish were taken in this one section over five hours than would have been caught all day going through my usual routine of "cherry-picking" the good water. Needless to say, I discovered a new favorite way to nymph that day.

French nymphing is successful because the angler is not relying on matching a hatch or a certain insect; instead, he's relying on reaction strikes. This means that the fly descends to the streambed, and, because of the use of a tungsten bead and fluorescent materials in the fly dressing, the trout will take the fly because the fly triggers a reaction. The quick upstream casting is done to make the fish react positively to the nymph and eat it when the fly enters its window. I have observed that the majority of my takes occur before the nymph reaches the bottom. This reaffirms my hypothesis that the trout takes the fly because it reacts. After all, what nymph descends through the water column as opposed to ascending?

Equipment

For French nymphing, I like to use a ten- or eleven-foot, three- or four-weight rod. A soft tip protects the light tippets that are frequently used. In addition to the soft tip, make sure that the rod has a stiff butt section that is capable of transmitting power through the rod. This will make it easy to turn over the long, fine leaders and light nymphs commonly used with this technique. Because of the longer rod length, be sure to

The author is about to net a fish in some heavier current. Notice that he is going to net the fish in the slower water created by his wake in the stream. Don't try to net fish in heavy current, as you run the risk of losing them. JUSTIN IDE

use a reel that is one size larger than the rated line weight; this will balance out the rod. A balanced rod and reel will cause less fatigue and make for a more enjoyable day on the water; this is critical, as these methods frequently require the use of an extended arm.

Leader Sections

Butt Section

The leaders can be anywhere from fifteen to eighteen feet in length. The entire leader, except for the last five to eight feet, is composed of a heavier butt section. I start off my butt section with a thirty-inch piece of stiff .021-inch RIO Powerflex. This is followed by twenty inches of .019-inch, then fifteen inches of both .017-inch and .015-inch. The last section is ten inches of .013-inch. This heavy butt section allows the angler to turn over the flies with ease. Since this method is fished with very long leaders, which are tapered down to some fine tippets, the butt section plays an important role in delivering the flies properly.

After the butt section comes the sighter, which is an in-line strike indicator. The sighter is followed by the tippet, to which the flies are tied. This final piece of the leader can be anywhere from four to ten feet, depending on the water depth and velocity.

Sighter or Indicator

The sighter is a device used to aid in strike detection. It can be fished as an in-line indicator when raised off the water or, when laid on the water, as a floating indicator. The sighter is actually in direct contact with the flies at all times. There should be no slack or any dead spot in your rigging—one reason why this method is so deadly. Any take is transmitted directly to the sighter, which is easily visible to the angler. Sighters can be made or purchased in a variety of ways.

When using monofilament for the sighter, there are two options: a straight piece of brightly colored monofilament or a curly whirly, also known as a coiled sighter. A curly whirly is a short length of monofilament prepared by the angler to have spring-like curls. The mono holds the curls when prepared correctly. All that is needed to make a coiled sighter is a pen, two rubber O-rings, and your monofilament. You take the monofilament (Golden Stren or high-vis Ande) and attach it to the pen. Next, you wind it up the pen, cut the excess, and place the pen in boiling water for five minutes. When you are finished, take it out and place it in the freezer overnight. (In addition to the Stren and Ande, Jan Siman and Umpqua also make bicolor indicator material, which consists of fluorescent yellow and orange. The contrasting colors can make it much easier to detect strikes, especially under varying light conditions.)

When it's tied onto your leader, if the curls unravel or hesitate while drifting downstream, you may have a strike. When tying sighters to your leader, you can either tie a small perfection loop onto both ends or use tippet rings, which are readily available at most fly shops.

In addition to the coiled sighter, a straight sighter can also work, especially when fishing heavier flies where you don't need the sensitivity of a coiled indicator.

Rigging

Once you have tied your butt section, rigging the rest of your leader system is quite easy. Coming off the butt section, tie in the sighter followed by the tippet. Simple clinch knots tied to the loops on each end can be used to attach both the butt section and tippets to the sighter. Water type dictates how you should be fishing your nymphs. If you are fishing a deep, fast run, you will generally need less tippet than you would when fishing a fast, shallow riffle. The smaller the flies, the lighter the tippet. I often use 6X Fluoroflex Plus. The smaller-diameter tippet lessens the drag of the current and allows you to reach the bottom with some surprisingly small flies.

When using heavier flies in situations where getting the offerings down is not an issue, I generally use 5X but sometimes as heavy as 4X if bottom snags and/or big fish are common. The length of the tippet is generally twice the depth of the water that you are going to be fishing. For example, if I am going to be fishing a section of stream that has an average water depth of three feet, I will use six feet of tippet to my first nymph.

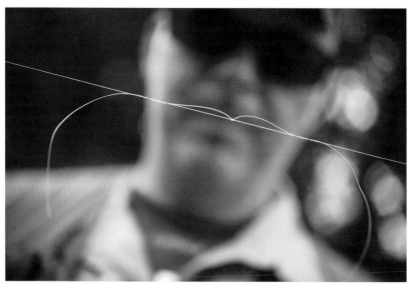

A surgeon's knot is the quickest way to tie on a dropper. Tie the nymph on the end facing away from the rod. Cut the tag end pointing back toward the rod. The length of the dropper tag should be between four and six inches. JUSTIN IDE

European Leader

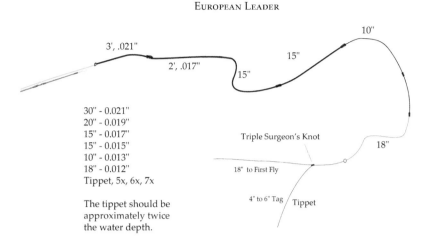

30" - 0.021"
20" - 0.019"
15" - 0.017"
15" - 0.015"
10" - 0.013"
18" - 0.012"
Tippet, 5x, 6x, 7x

The tippet should be
approximately twice
the water depth.

When tying on flies, make sure they are tied onto droppers. A *dropper* is a piece of line that comes off your leader and is usually the tag end of a triple surgeon's knot. After the initial piece of tippet is attached to the sighter, I tie my first dropper to the other end of the tippet attached to the sighter. This is done simply by taking another piece of tippet, about thirty inches in length, and tying it to the leader using a triple surgeon's knot.

After tying the knot, clip the top tag, which is the tag end of the knot going toward the sighter. Tying the fly to the top tag end could possibly cause the knot to fail when hooking a fish, although some people prefer to use it because they believe it reduces tangles by making your dropper fly stand out away from the main leader. The downward pointing tag (toward your leader tip) will be the piece of leader to which your top dropper fly gets tied. The top dropper fly is usually the one that is lightest, possibly even unweighted. The tag end should be four to six inches in length to allow for fly changes; to give the fly freedom of movement; and also to create just enough slack for the trout to successfully inhale your nymph. Also, make sure that you have about twenty inches between your flies. Your heavier anchor fly is your point fly, the last fly in your setup, on the terminal end of your leader. This is not always the case, but the heavier fly is often fished at the point.

Do yourself a favor and learn to tie your flies on with a Davy knot. Not only is it the quickest, easiest knot out there, but with practice, it only uses up a fraction of an inch of tippet each time you tie it. This will allow you a surprising number of fly changes before you have to redo your rigging. This is important, as you will be frequently changing to heavier or lighter anchor flies as the water speed and depth change. The break strength of this knot is quite good too. I've landed quite a few Great Lakes steelhead over ten pounds on 4X to 5X tippet using the Davy knot.

Presentation

There are two ways to present your flies when executing a long-leader, Euro-nymphing technique: directly upstream (classic French style) or across and slightly upstream (Spanish style).

The author fishes long-leader, French/Spanish style. Notice the bow in the line and the outstretched arm. This is the proper position for fishing these styles of nymphing.
JUSTIN IDE

No matter how you choose to present your flies, the rod angle at the end of the cast is critical. The rod must stop dead and cannot drop below ten o'clock. Utilizing a tuck cast, at the end of the drift, bring the rod slightly back to allow the flies to come back at you and dive straight through the water column. This enables your flies to quickly reach the desired depth. At times the trout will take your flies as soon as they hit the water; this is because they are reacting to something foreign coming into their field of view. This technique allows the long leader to unfurl and straighten out, providing direct contact to your flies the second they hit the water. With traditional methods, many strikes go undetected in the first few feet of your drift.

When fishing upstream, you are not going to be making long drifts. This presentation is more ideally suited for shallow pocket water, where the lies are much smaller, and where the water you are fishing is shallow enough to approach the pocket from straight downstream. Position yourself directly behind or slightly off to the side of the lie. As you cast, keep the rod up and track your flies toward you. Once your rod reaches the twelve o'clock position, snap your wrist to pull the flies out of the water, and make another cast. This is known as "rapid-fire" casting, because many casts are made in a short period, covering a section of water quite thoroughly. Make sure to not wade through the water until you have fished it. Walk upstream in a methodical way. Grid out the water in front of you, making sure that no lie goes untouched. Feather your casts out from left to right, and then move a few steps upriver and repeat the sequence.

For the cross-stream presentation, I like to position myself directly across from where the fish are holding. Assuming that straight upstream is twelve o'clock, the flies are cast at two o'clock. They are then drifted slightly below my position in the stream, which would be three-thirty or four o'clock. The only exception might be during heavy hatching activity, wherein the flies might be allowed to swing below my position. This style of nymphing can be extremely effective during a caddis hatch or a hatch of other active insects, such as Isonychia. When I cast my flies, I keep the rod up to gain tension and stay in contact with the flies.

I do this in case I get a strike before my flies reach the "prime lie" that I am fishing. This approach is extremely effective in low-gradient riffles and deep, fast water. I make adjustments according to the conditions: In deep, fast water, I use a heavy anchor fly and lengthen out the tippet section. Shallower or slower water dictates a lighter anchor fly and maybe a shorter tippet.

Leading the Flies (Contact)

Anglers accustomed to fishing with indicators may have to get used to leading the flies. Unlike indicator nymphing, where an angler uses controlled slack to achieve a dead drift, French nymphers use constant tension to control the drift and to detect strikes. *Leading* refers to keeping some degree of tension on your leader and flies while moving the rod tip ahead and downstream of where your leader cuts into the water's surface. Doing this keeps you in touch with your flies, enabling detection of even the lightest takes, as well as keeping your flies drifting along without snagging the bottom. Only experience will teach you how much

As soon as the cast is made, the rod is in the up position, arm outstretched, ready to lead the nymphs as they drift downstream. JUSTIN IDE

tension to keep on your leader and at what speed to track your rod tip downstream. Lead too slow and you will create slack, which will cause you to miss strikes and hang on the bottom. Too fast, and your drift will be unnatural and you won't get many hits. It's a very subtle balancing act. The trout will let you know when you have it right.

Recommended Flies

Weighted nymphs are key to this technique. I take my favorite trout nymphs and modify them by adding lead underbodies and tungsten beads. One common denominator here is that the vast majority of flies used in long-leader Euro-nymphing are slim-bodied, with little or no appendages to stop them from sinking. Almost all of my nymphs used for this technique consist of a Coq De Leon tail, an abdomen, and a collar of fluorescent dubbed material. I also commonly use fluorescent beads or thread hot spots.

Keep in mind that the flies used for these techniques need not be heavy. When fished in shallow water, a smaller, lighter nymph will have sufficient weight to get down into the zone, whereas a heavy fly will

In the author's dropper nymph box, notice that the flies are smaller in size. They range mostly from size 12 to 22 and imitate various types of in-stream insects. JUSTIN IDE

sink too fast and get hung up. In addition to the lead wire and tungsten beads, these flies are very slim and are designed to achieve great depth with the smallest amount of weight possible.

Conclusion

Having a correct method of presenting flies in every water type should be the goal of every angler. French and Spanish nymphing enable an angler to fish nymphs in a variety of water types that are otherwise not easily fished. I have watched many anglers walk past some very good holding lies simply because they did not have the correct setup to fish that water. While these techniques do not work in every single nymphing situation, they are quite versatile and will give you something new to add to your arsenal. If practiced regularly, they can be quite productive.

One last beginner's hint: Carry lots of tippet. Don't waste your time trying to untangle ten cents' worth of line. If you can't get your flies untangled in ten seconds, cut them off and retie. You'll have more time to spend fishing rather than untangling!

CHAPTER 5

Dry Flies

Introduction

For many anglers, dry-fly fishing is the pinnacle of the sport. Casting dry flies to surface-feeding trout is indeed exciting. It's exhilarating to watch a large trout's nose come up out of the water to take your fly.

When fishing dry flies, it pays to take your time and really look over a piece of water. Sometimes the largest trout make the tiniest rises. Never walk into the river and just start casting. Have a game plan. JUSTIN IDE

Like nymph fishing, there are various methods used to fish dry flies. On small streams, you are not able to present your flies the same way you would on a larger stream. The trout behave differently in different habitats. Small-stream trout, for instance, are often less selective. When fishing larger rivers and streams, an angler needs to take a different approach, matching insects more carefully and paying greater attention to presentation.

TACKLE

If I had to choose two rods to cover most dry-fly fishing situations, they would be a nine-foot, three-weight and a nine-foot, five-weight. Of course there are some specialized rods for small streams that can be as short as six feet in length, but for most trout fishing on streams from twenty to sixty feet wide, a nine-foot rod is the ticket. The line weight for those rods depends on the tippet size. For example, if I'm fishing a lot of 6X and 7X Powerflex and Suppleflex tippet and smaller flies (size 16 down to 20), I will generally use a 3-weight line. If I were to fish larger dry flies, and in windy conditions, I'd use the 5-weight. The 5-weight is ideal for fishing tippet sizes of 3X to 5X and larger flies from sizes 6 to 14.

When choosing the right size leader for dry-fly fishing, anglers need to consider the size of the fly they'll be presenting, as well as the scenario in which they'll be fishing. If you're going to be fishing in a spring creek to more-selective, wary trout, you should use a longer leader, from twelve to fifteen feet, tapered down to 6X or 7X. Conversely, if fishing on a small mountain stream, a seven-and-a-half to nine-foot tapered leader is usually just fine.

When adding tippet onto your leader, remember that the average leader has about twenty to thirty inches of tippet attached to the butt section. When adding additional tippet, it is generally a good idea to cut off eighteen inches or so from the end of your leader and then add the amount of tippet that you desire.

For example, if I were going to be fishing dry flies to rising fish on flat, calm water, I might take a fifteen-foot-long tapered leader, which would be tapered down to 6X, and from there I would cut off about eighteen inches of the 6X and attach three feet of 7X to the end of the leader. Then I would attach my dry fly. If you were to attach the piece of 7X right to the end of the twenty to thirty inches of 6X, you would lose the energy transfer that the powerful, stiff butt section gives you. This would hinder the ability of the leader to straighten out at the end of the cast. This is one of the reasons why many anglers get frustrated with longer leaders. When adding tippet, you have to take some of the old off before putting on the new.

For dry flies, line choice is extremely important. When fishing to spooky fish on low-gradient streams, a RIO Trout LT DT is an excellent choice, especially in the lower line weights. As the need to cast my flies farther becomes more important, a RIO Gold is my preferred line.

Leader Additives

When fishing longer leaders, always make sure to degrease your tippet. For this application I like to use Loon Outdoors Snake River Mud. To my knowledge, this is the only company producing this type of product. Degreasing the leader removes any grease or lubricant from the line. Many anglers will make a great presentation only to have the trout reject the fly because of sunlight reflecting off the leader. This simple step will take that possibility out of the equation.

For the rest of the leader, grease it up with a paste-type floatant. Watery floatants have a tendency to come off easily and need to be reapplied constantly. Doing this will allow your leader to stay above the surface of the water and will cause less drag. This will also make it easier to pick up the line and recast. Apply the same floatant to the first five feet of fly line.

Always be sure to have fly floatant and a fly drier with you. Most companies make comparable products in this category. Having a dry fly that is actually dry is always a good thing! Coat the fly with floatant before use, and use the drier to dry the fly out as needed. The drier eliminates the need for numerous false casts, which can often spook fish, especially on bright, sunny days.

Methods of Presentation

The author casts dry flies to trout rising to Tricos. During the summer, trout will seek areas where they have refuge from the bright sun. You will often find them in shade created by trees. HEATH POTTER

There are several methods of presentation when fishing dry flies. An *upstream presentation* is generally used on streams so small that standing across from, or upstream of, the fish would spook it. A *down-and-across presentation* is better on larger rivers, such as the Henry's Fork of the Snake River or New York's West Branch of the Delaware River. These two rivers are very large, and if the angler takes the time to get in position, the likelihood of spooking the trout is slim. A down-and-across presentation on bigger water also lets the fly pass over the fish before the leader does.

Another method of presenting dry flies is to use what's called a *puddle cast.* This is effective for fishing a medium-size stream with a trout rising directly below your position. Turn your shoulders toward your target and make your cast. On your forward cast, take your rod and, right before the fly is set to land, jerk the rod back toward you. Once you are finished doing this, drop the rod down. You will see lots

The author makes an upstream cast with some slack in the line to allow for a drag-free drift. JUSTIN IDE

of S curves in your line. These allow your fly to drift without dragging in the current.

Prospecting

When fishing small rivers and streams, standing behind the fish gives you a sure advantage, keeping you out of the trout's line of vision. Their eyes are in the front of their head; therefore, they are unable to see the angler who is behind them, wading with caution.

On smaller streams, *prospecting*—searching with dry flies—is an excellent approach. We have spoken multiple times about how trout in small streams are more opportunistic. They are highly susceptible to being caught on dry flies. The best way to prospect the smaller stream is to work your way upstream, making your casts all upstream of your position. As you cast, you want to make presentations to every likely lie created by seams in the current. It's also important to cast right along the bank, especially if the stream has larger boulders and structure, such as fallen trees or other debris. Banks create excellent holding habitat for

When all else fails, consider using a terrestrial, which will fool some of the toughest-to-catch trout. JUSTIN IDE

trout. My favorite dry flies to prospect with are stimulators, hoppers (especially out west), large buoyant caddis patterns, and terrestrials, especially larger beetles and ants.

You can also prospect on larger rivers and streams. Take the largest insect that might be hatching at the time, or falling into the water from the banks, and cast upstream into all the likely holding water. Out west, hoppers and stimulators, as well as other foam-bodied dry flies, make for excellent searching patterns. I remember one specific summer when I was fishing on the Madison River in the morning, and there were lots of golden stoneflies hatching. Rather than nymphing, I walked up the bank with a yellow stimulator and took dozens of trout.

Small- to Medium-Size Rivers and Streams

There are numerous ways to present dry flies to trout on small- to medium-size rivers. If there are trout rising, you can cast your dry flies right to them. You can use an upstream cast if you are below the fish, a puddle cast if you are above the fish, or, if you are stealthy enough, there are times when you can make a down-and-across presentation. In addition to fishing to actively rising trout, you can also prospect on smaller streams. To prospect, use flies that match the insects that are hatching, or are going to be hatching, that day. The biomass of these streams is generally higher than in headwater streams, so the fish become accustomed to eating certain food sources; your fly should match those closely. If there are tan caddis hatching, for instance, a favorite searching pattern of mine would be Craig Mathews's X-Caddis. In the East we have the Isonychia mayfly, sometimes called the slate drake. These flies hatch from June all the way to October on many of our streams. Dry flies that match this hatch can be extremely productive, especially when used as a searching pattern.

Spring Creeks

When fishing spring creeks, remember that these trout can be very spooky. Knowing their behavior is often more critical than selecting the right fly. On these streams, your fly size can be off slightly; however, both your approach and cast need to be perfect. The best way to fish for rising trout on a spring creek is to approach them from a downstream position. Often I will stay off the bank by at least a rod's length. I was fishing the Letort a few years back when sunlight hit the tip of my rod. That reflection of sunlight, believe it or not, was enough to alert numerous trout to the fact that I was at the stream. Fish ceased rising, and I saw a number of wakes from trout that I had spooked.

Don't go to a spring creek expecting to have the best day of your life. Expect to catch only a few fish, but know that you will have earned every single one of them.

Large Rivers and Tailwaters

Picture this: Draw an imaginary fifty- to sixty-foot circle around the trout that you want to catch. When fishing larger rivers, you can approach the fish anywhere, so long as you stand outside of this circle. The two most productive spots to approach trout in this scenario are

The author is holding a large brown trout which took a down and across presentation with a long leader and light tippet. Large trout like this one can regularly be taken on dry flies if the correct angle or presentation is used. HEATH POTTER

casting at a 45-degree angle downstream and casting at the same angle upstream, toward the fish. Casting from these angles allows you to keep the leader from passing over the trout before the fly.

Many anglers swear that the down-and-across at a 45-degree angle is the best presentation. The rationale for this is that the tails of the fly pass over the trout before the rest of the fly. However, after witnessing thousands of hatches and rising fish, I believe the way your fly floats down the river need only be free of any resistance from surface currents. As long as the fly matches the emerging insects, it can be floating forwards, backwards, or sideways, so long as it is riding undisturbed in the current.

When fishing on heavily pressured streams or rivers with wild, wary fish, your goal is to get within fifty to sixty feet of the fish you are casting to. If you get closer than this, especially in slower water, just moving your body to change flies and tippet can cause enough disturbance to stop the fish from rising.

Never neglect side channels, the small rivulets that come off the main river channel. Some large fish can be found in them. A dry fly presented upstream can be extremely effective in these small areas. JUSTIN IDE

Matching the Hatch

In the author's dry-fly box, there are various imitations of the insects hatching during the time when the photograph was taken: emergers, adult, and spinner imitations.
JUSTIN IDE

To catch large wild trout on dry flies, you need to exercise extreme patience. Watching the water prior to fishing it is vital to locating any trophy fish that are surface-feeding. And don't limit your attention to the best lies; large trout often will take up residence in extremely shallow lies to feed on emerging insects. By carefully observing the water, you will see that there are large fish feeding where you wouldn't even think a juvenile should be. Why? The fish feel safe there because no one bothers to look at those locales. They only look for the prime lies. Remember as well that sometimes the largest fish will cause the smallest surface disturbance. What might look like a thumb coming out of the water might be the nose of a two-foot-plus brown trout.

During heavy hatches in particular, the largest trout on the stream will often hold in the skinniest water. They do this because this is where they can get the maximum amount of food. It's kind of like a pecking order. The larger fish go to the front of the line, while the smaller fish are behind them. This is the case in riffled water. When fishing in tailouts, the larger fish can be found almost anywhere. Generally, tailouts are where I catch my largest fish on dry flies. I think this is due to the fact that they can move into the tailout from where they are holding and, if

The author's favorite dry-fly combination for evening-into-dark dry-fly fishing is a large white Wulff with a spinner tied to the bend of the hook, twenty inches from the larger fly. ALEJANDRO GOMEZ

spooked, can go right back to their holding lie.

The simplest way to try to match insects is to think of what the fish see from underneath the surface. I match hatching insects by using the following three criteria: size, shape, and color. Many of the dry flies that are commercially tied are extremely well dressed and look great to our eyes. However, the trout see the flies very differently. When a trout looks up at the fly, all it sees is a body and a silhouette of a wing. The body of

This trout fell for a sulphur emerger during a heavy hatch. Trout that ignore adult imitations will sometimes readily take an emerger. TOM WALSH

the fly appears to be carrot-shaped, due to the increase in diameter from the tail to the thorax of the fly.

The trout can also tell what color the fly is to some degree. There are various theories on this. Some say that trout can see only in shades of color, and others say that they can see the exact color. I believe the latter to some extent, especially when there is a heavy emergence of insects and the trout are feeding heavily on them. I like to use flies like the Comparadun or the Compara-Emerger. Flies like John Barr's Vis-A-Dun are also extremely effective. The same is true for flies that imitate caddisflies and stoneflies. The imitations that match the underside of the naturals the best are often the ones that are the most productive.

The next important thing to match is the length of the fly. An extremely selective fish might ignore an imitation that is shorter or longer than the naturals. Having an imitation that matches the length, taper, and color of the naturals is essential to having success when dry-fly fishing. Additionally, knowing the correct stage in which the insect is feeding on is equally important, whether it be an emerger, adult, or spinner.

Right before dark, it's tough to beat fishing a spinner that is either yellow or rusty in color, depending on the prevailing hatch of insects. JUSTIN IDE

CHAPTER 6

Dry/Dropper Fishing

Introduction

There are times when trout might be actively feeding but presenting nymphs on the streambed is not the best option. If I see even one trout opportunistically rise to take a dry fly, I'll usually change my setup to a

The author prepares to fish a low-gradient riffle with a dry/dropper combination.
JUSTIN IDE

dry/dropper. These situations usually present themselves during periods of low water. When the streams are low and clear, trout will be more likely to feed on the surface. This technique of fishing excels when fishing on spring creeks, low-gradient riffled water, and smaller freestone streams.

Streams where trout are subjected to high angling pressure are also generally well suited for dry/dropper techniques. This is an extremely delicate style of presenting nymphs under a dry fly. In many of these streams, the trout are spooky enough that anglers need to present their nymphs at a distance in order to be successful. The only way to do this is to suspend them under dry flies. When fishing with the correct leader system, dry flies and small nymphs can increase your catch rates, even in some surprisingly tough conditions.

When fishing in low flows, anglers need to suspend the nymphs in the water column. And if fishing in shallow, riffled water, there's a greater chance of snagging on the bottom if nymphing with split shot. Using one or two lightly weighted flies under a dry fly lessens the chance of getting snagged; the nymphs ride right across the tops of the rocks. Dry/dropper fishing also works well in areas where the stream is slow and deep. In slower water, nymphs have a greater chance of getting caught on the bottom due to the fact that there is little resistance from surface currents, allowing the nymphs to sink more easily. Suspending the flies is necessary in slow-water zones. Fishing in weedy spring-creek scenarios also calls for keeping the flies out of the weeds and in plain view of the fish; dry/dropper combinations allow you to do just that.

Dry/dropper combinations work especially well during mayfly and caddisfly hatches. Many of these nymphs and pupae are vulnerable near the surface, and trout will frequently hold right below the surface in order to feed, looking up to take potential food items. Placing one or two lightly weighted nymphs below a dry fly can be extremely effective in taking these opportunistic trout. The dry/dropper technique also allows anglers to cover a large amount of water without moving their feet. You can get out of the riffle and work different areas just by adjusting the length of your casts.

TACKLE FOR VARIOUS SCENARIOS

When fishing a dry/dropper system, it's important to match the tackle with the situation. For example, if you're throwing a hopper/dropper nymph combination, you won't use the same rod as if you were fishing a smaller dry/dropper on a small stream. You use a heavier rod to cast large flies. This is extremely important, especially out west, where the majority of streams have extremely large quantities of grasshoppers along the shore, and trout frequently feed opportunistically on them during the summer months, especially from late July on. My favorite rod for this type of fishing is a nine-foot, four- to six-weight. This rod will enable an angler to cast large dry/dropper combinations, even in heavy wind, which is frequently the case on larger Western rivers and streams. The leader and tippet used are generally much heavier: Twelve-foot 3X or 4X Powerflex leaders attached to the dry fly are common, and 4X to 5X Fluoroflex Plus is generally used to connect the nymph to the dry fly. You have to match your tackle to the water. When fishing dry/dropper on larger streams or in windy situations, upsizing your tackle to match conditions will enable you to effectively fish the larger, more-bulky, and often harder-to-cast dry/dropper combinations.

When fishing dry/dropper on smaller streams, or where fish are spookier, scale down your tackle. If you're fishing on a gentle or low-gradient spring creek, you will find a nine-foot, three- or four-weight rod necessary to present the flies. You'll need to present your dry/dropper combinations with more finesse. Rods with lighter fly lines generally cause less commotion on the surface, spooking fewer fish. In addition, thirteen-and-a-half-foot Suppleflex leaders tapered down to 5X and 6X are commonly used when fishing to spooky fish. The fluorocarbon tippet used can range anywhere from 6X to 8X, depending on the clarity of the stream.

When fishing larger flies on heavier rods, I like to use a RIO Grand in a weight-forward. This line has a very aggressive front taper, which does an excellent job cutting through the wind in order to turn the large, bulky flies over. When fishing smaller streams and spring creeks, a Trout LT weight-forward is an excellent choice. This line is suppler and matches up perfectly in situations where you need a line that will present your flies more delicately.

Rigging

For my main section of leader, from the fly line to the dry fly, I like to use a leader stiff enough to turn over the dry/dropper system. These leaders will be rated anywhere from 3X to 6X, depending on the scenario. Use a heavier leader for larger dry flies and a lighter leader for smaller dry flies.

DRY/DROPPER

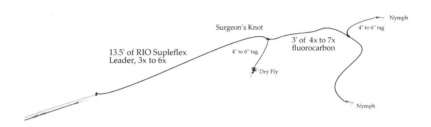

I like to tie my dry flies on dropper tags, allowing my dry fly to fish in a more-natural manner. I prefer not to tie the tags off the bend of the hook, because the drag of the leader is on one end of the dry fly and the drag from the nymph is on the other. Having the tippet attached to only the hook eye eliminates up to half of the possible drag.

After attaching the leader to the fly line, I tie a surgeon's knot onto the end of the leader with a thirty-inch piece of 4X to 5X fluorocarbon for larger flies, or 6X to 7X when fishing to spooky fish or in low-water scenarios. When fishing subsurface, I prefer to use fluorocarbon because it is abrasion-resistant and less visible beneath the water. After attaching the fluorocarbon, cut the tag end that points back toward the fly line. The remaining tag end should be four to six inches in length. The dry fly will be tied onto this tag end. I tie my nymph about twenty-four to thirty inches behind my dry fly, enabling me to effectively fish water up to eighteen inches in depth.

Dry/Dropper, One Nymph

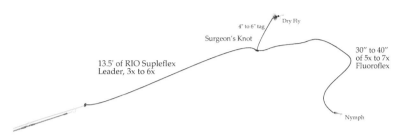

Dry Fly

4" to 6" tag

Surgeon's Knot

30" to 40"
of 5x to 7x
Fluoroflex

13.5' of RIO Supleflex
Leader, 3x to 6x

Nymph

When fishing in water deeper than eighteen inches, I commonly use two nymphs rather than one. Again, both the dry fly and the first nymph are tied on dropper tags. I cut off the first nymph and tie another surgeon's knot to the end of the fluorocarbon; then I cut off the tag end pointing toward the dry fly. I attach one nymph on the first tag end and another nymph at the end of the leader. The nymphs are typically spaced twenty to twenty-four inches apart.

Fishing a Dry/Dropper in High, Fast Streams

When fishing dry/dropper combinations in higher-gradient streams, recall how you prospected upstream with dry flies. The difference here

In the author's dry/dropper box, notice the large, buoyant dry flies on the top side of the box. On the plain magnetic side are the dropper nymphs, which are tied with tungsten beads to achieve depth. ALEJANDRO GOMEZ

is that in addition to changing the style of the dry fly, you will also be fishing either a single or tandem nymph below your dry fly. This decision is made primarily based upon water depth. If the water is between one and two feet in depth, you will want to use one nymph. If the water is over two feet in depth, with moderate current, two nymphs might be beneficial. A major bonus to using two nymphs is that you are not only covering the surface and raising the opportunistic trout to the dry fly but are also covering multiple levels in the water column. When fishing in this manner, cast your dry/dropper system directly upstream of your position. Once the cast is made, immediately begin stripping in the line as it floats toward you. Be careful not to allow the line to go below your rod tip as you are stripping. This would make your dry fly drag toward your position, causing your nymphs to ascend to the water's surface rather than staying on the bottom, where they belong.

Fishing a Dry/Dropper in Difficult Situations

When fishing a dry/dropper in difficult situations, especially on spring creeks, keep a low profile streamside. You don't want the trout to be

A dry/dropper works in many scenarios. In this case, there were several fish cruising around in the tailout of a pool. Fishing tandem nymphs below a dry fly can entice even the wariest trout. JUSTIN IDE

aware of your presence. When fishing spring creeks, I like to observe the stream and its currents before making my first cast, and I like to stay between five and ten feet away from the bank of the stream. This will give me room to present my flies while not allowing the fish to know that I am there. In addition to keeping a low profile, it is important to move slowly when fishing these systems. Quick movements look very unnatural. The key here is to blend into your surroundings. I often find myself wearing various shades of olive and tan depending on the season and waters fished.

Fishing in Larger Rivers

When fishing a dry/dropper in larger rivers, your approach does not need to be as stealthy as it would be in smaller streams and spring creeks, but this doesn't mean that you can simply plunge right into the river, either. Take your time getting in position to make the cast. One summer on the Madison River in Montana, fishing two small tungsten

Never think that a trout will not take the dry fly when fishing dry/dropper. Here's a twenty-four-inch trout that fell for a Hi-Vis Klinkhammer dry fly. TOM WALSH

nymphs under a Chernobyl Ant in slack water along the bank, the fish were not only taking the nymphs but quite a few came up and exploded on the dry fly as well. Up until this point I did not have much faith in this system of fishing. I generally fished either dry flies or various nymphing techniques for the majority of my angling.

Another scenario where a dry/dropper rig performs well is on low-gradient riffled water on larger watersheds, like the Delaware and Missouri. In some areas of these streams, the water might be anywhere from six to eighteen inches in depth. Fishing a larger attractor dry fly with smaller attractor nymphs allows you to present your flies from a distance in areas where the fish are extremely wary due to the stream being low-gradient. I've attempted to fish these same locations with indicator nymphing methods and did not do well. Fishing nymphs suspended under attractor dry flies is more productive. In deeper water, however, indicators typically outproduce a dry/dropper.

Presentation of the Flies

When casting a dry/dropper rig, be sure to employ a swift power stroke on the forward cast with an abrupt stop of the rod at the two o'clock position. These two steps will allow the leader to unfurl and lay out the dry fly and nymphs in a straight line. This is essential to detecting strikes that occur as the nymphs descend to the stream bottom.

When fishing a dry/dropper, I usually place myself at the beginning of the section I am going to fish. This means that if I am fishing riffled water, I will start fishing right where the pool begins. In this position, I will be below the fish that I'm targeting.

After I am in proper position, I establish a plan of attack before casting. I look at the water and make mental notes of the various depths that I'll be fishing. I also try to figure out where the best spot in the section will be and plan a strategy on how to fish my way up to that spot while causing the least amount of disturbance. I don't want to spook the trout.

Fishing dry/dropper combinations in shallow, low-gradient riffles is very effective. Here the author is hooked into a nice wild brown trout. JUSTIN IDE

Once I have surveyed the section, I set up my leader and flies. I decide where I'm going to cast and how many casts I'm going to make in each section in order to most efficiently and effectively cover the stream. Once I make these decisions, I begin to work that section of stream. I never go into a section of stream without a plan of attack.

CHAPTER 7

Streamers

Introduction

Streamer fishing, much like bass fishing, can be quite exciting. The takes from the fish are often vicious, and the tugs you get when a trout takes your fly are simply amazing. In addition to the fish that you bring to

The author launches a cast at a bank in hopes of coming up with something large.
DAVE LATTNER

97

hand, some of the chases, often from abnormally large fish, will leave you with your heart beating out of your chest. When the right conditions for streamers arise, fly fishers should take advantage of them; fishing streamers properly, either while wading or from a boat, can yield the largest fish of the season.

Cloud cover provides excellent opportunities for streamer fishing, as the reduced amount of ambient light makes the trout feel safer. Safety leads to aggressive feeding. They will move out of their lies to take a streamer. Lower light will also camouflage your streamer, making it look more like a natural food source. Another scenario where a streamer is especially effective would be during a rainstorm. The cloud cover and ensuing commotion caused by rain hitting the surface of the water distort the trout's view of things outside of their world. When this happens, coupled with the obvious cloud cover, streamer fishing can be exceptional. Weather fronts and changes are generally associated with rain. Trout will often feed aggressively ahead of a passing front. Finally, streamer fishing is also good during high-water events. Whether the water is high and stained, or even high and clear, the trout will be aggressive. They are more likely to move from their "safe" holding lies and expose themselves to take your streamer. Your streamer moves water and causes wakes, which the trout feel in their lateral line. The aggression caused by water receding after a high-water event can make for some great streamer fishing.

A good rule of thumb when choosing to fish streamers is that any change in weather or stream conditions generally brings about good streamer fishing.

TACKLE: ROD, REEL, AND LINES

The tackle for streamer fishing is similar for both boat and wade fishing. When streamer-fishing, the ideal rods are nine to nine and a half feet long and rated for 6- or 7-weight fly lines. Many anglers like to use a nine-foot rod when streamer-fishing. I prefer to use a nine-and-a-half-foot rod. I feel that the extra six inches gives you a little extra wiggle

This nice fall brown trout was taken on a Rattlesnake streamer on Montana's Madison River. JUSTIN MASSIMO

at the tip of the rod and enables you to impart more motion into your streamers while stripping them in.

Fast-action rods are also good. The stiff butt section of the rod drives the larger hook into a trout's jaw. Trout caught while streamer-fishing are generally larger than the fish you are attempting to catch when using other methods. Large trout have thicker jaws, adapted to feeding on minnows and other fish. Often several hook sets are needed to firmly plant the streamer into the jaw of the fish. A rod with a stiff butt section greatly aids in the ability to get better hook sets. A slower-action rod with less backbone will result in less-effective hook sets and more fish coming off after the initial hook set.

The reel is an important part of your tackle when streamer-fishing. Look for a reel with a good disk drag, preferably one that is sealed as well. Since you will, at times, be fishing streamers under harsh conditions, it is important to have a reel that can handle the elements. And if you are fortunate enough to hook into the trout of a lifetime, having a premium drag can be a lifesaver. A good streamer reel should also have a large arbor. This will help because as the line comes off, it will not retain small coils, which can cause tangles in the line. This is commonly the case with streamers, especially when making long casts and retrieves.

And speaking of retrieves: Be watchful as to where you put your line as you strip in your flies. Many anglers will use what is called a *stripping basket* in order to avoid tangles. There is nothing worse than hooking a large trout and having the hook pull out due to a tangle. Believe me, I have learned this the hard way through firsthand experience.

The lines used for streamer fishing vary greatly. When wade-fishing, a floating line is acceptable for the majority of scenarios. But for those times when the water is deeper, you can either add sink tips to the end of your floating line, or you can purchase a new sinking line. Many companies make fly lines with weighted heads. When fishing with streamers from a boat in slightly deeper waters, if the weight of the streamer itself is not enough to get it down through the water column, a 150-grain sink-tip streamer line is my preferred line. In extreme circumstances I will fish a 200-grain Density Compensated streamer line. This line will get your streamers down quickly, particularly during lower to moderate flows.

The water depths, velocity, fly size, and weight dictate the line that you will need. If you are casting into shallow water with flies that do not have a large profile, a 150-grain sinking line might be perfect. Conversely, if you were to use a larger-profile streamer, you might need a 200-grain sinking line to get that streamer down through the water column. For the majority of your streamer fishing, a 150- to 200-grain sinking line will be all that you need.

There are also some scenarios where the use of certain lines will overlap. If you are fishing in shallow water and want to use an extremely rapid retrieve, you might want to forgo the intermediate or 150-grain line in favor of a 200-grain line, which will keep the fly down in the water column even with a faster rate of retrieve. If the fish want a slower speed of retrieve, go with a 150-grain line even if the water is deep. A slow retrieve combined with a 200-grain line will often cause your

This large trout fell victim to a Galloup's Articulated Butt Monkey streamer.
TOM WALSH

flies to get hung up on the bottom. It is important to play around with retrieve rates, as quite often the fish will prefer one to another.

Water temperatures can also play a role in how fast or slow your streamer retrieve should be. When water temperatures are in excess of 60 degrees (but not too hot), there are times when you cannot strip your streamers in quick enough. When the water temperatures are between 50 and 60 degrees, vary your retrieves. There are times when the trout will be more aggressive and will take a faster retrieve, and other times when the same fish will prefer a slower retrieve. As the water temperatures dip below the 50-degree mark, some trout can be taken on a faster retrieve; however, this generally occurs around spawning times, when the fish are more aggressive. Once the fish are done spawning and the water cools down, trout can be taken when streamers are swung in the deeper tailouts of pools. When the water

The author's largest trout to date was caught on a John Barr's Slumpbuster streamer.
TOM WALSH

temperatures dip below the 40-degree mark, swinging a streamer can become the best way to take the occasional fish.

There are certain situations that call for the use of what I consider specialty streamer lines. I fished the South Holston River in Tennessee a few times. This is a tailwater river wherein the flows are either extremely low or very high and fast. The use of an eight-weight rod and a 300-grain Density Compensated sinking line was necessary due to the size of the flies and the velocity of the current.

Rigging Up

Setting your tackle up for streamer fishing is quite simple. Most sinking lines do not come with a premade loop on the end of the fly line, so you'll need to nail-knot a foot-long piece of .017-inch monofilament to the end of your line. At the end of the new section of line, make a perfection loop. This is where you will attach your tippet. When fishing in extremely high water, 0X or 1X fluorocarbon is the tippet size to use. When fishing with smaller streamers, dropping the tippet to 2X or 3X can be beneficial. Keep in mind that the majority of the takes while fishing with streamers won't be subtle. The fish are not line-shy at all. Fishing with heavy tippets will keep your line from breaking due to the shock of a large fish taking your flies.

When fishing streamers on a sinking line, only a two- to three-foot piece of tippet is needed. However, when fishing streamers off of a floating line, a much longer tippet is appropriate; generally, four to six feet will put some degree of separation between the streamer and the floating fly line. This is what allows it to sink. Having too short of a tippet with a floating fly line will cut down on your streamer's ability to sink and will not allow your streamer to get to the fish.

How to Choose the Correct Streamer

Choosing a streamer can be a difficult task. There are so many options to choose from at your local fly shop, including thin-profiled streamers,

The author peeks into his box of streamers, attempting to make the correct choice based on water conditions. DAVE LATTNER

articulated streamers that are six to eight inches in length, and everything in between.

When choosing streamers to fish in clearer flows, I like to match the color to either the stream bottom or, if there are underwater weeds present, to the weeds. Baitfish are often camouflaged to either the color of weeds or the streambed. This keeps them safe from predators. Matching your streamers using this theory and then casting them into a likely holding area can make for some exciting angling. Large trout can be opportunistic, and casting a natural-looking streamer into an area where it should not be will often draw a strike from a trout that is just sitting there, waiting to pounce on an unsuspecting meal.

The second theory to apply when choosing a streamer occurs when the rivers are high and off-color. After a rain event or during snowmelt, trout will move from their usual holding areas and generally seek refuge along the banks in shallower water. This allows them to get out of the heavier current and more-turbid water. When the water is stained, the best visibility is along the banks. The trout take advantage of this. While

Articulated deer-hair streamers are effective in higher water or in turbulent, fast-moving water where creating a wake will entice a trout. JUSTIN IDE

High, dirty water can yield excellent results when fishing streamers. Here the author uses a 200-grain sinking line while fishing the shoreline. BOB CARPENTER

their vision is still not as keen as it is in clear water, it's certainly better than it would be if they were to stay in the center of the river. When fishing streamers during these scenarios, larger, articulated streamers, or streamers with large heads that move water, can be extremely effective. Since the trout's vision is compromised, they feed by using their limited sense of sight, as well as their uncanny ability to sense motion. Slim streamers that do not move water will often get ignored.

I like to use darker-colored streamers when water visibility is a foot or less; black, brown, or olive can be highly productive during periods when the water is turbid. These darker colors stand out from other objects that might be suspended throughout the water column. As the water clears, other colors such as yellow and white become more effective. On occasion, chartreuse has produced excellent results when the water is high and off-color. As the water begins to clear even further, more natural colors, such as tans and lighter shades of brown, can be deadly.

Wade-Fishing with Streamers

When wade-fishing with streamers (which generally means fishing in smaller streams), you want to present your streamers as if you were fishing nymphs upstream. Cast upstream and retrieve at a rate slightly faster than the current itself. You can also cast them to the banks if the water is off-color. If the water has good visibility, cast them into all of the places where a trout is likely to be holding under more-normal conditions. Make the casts no longer than fifty feet. If you are casting farther than fifty feet, simply change your position in the stream when it comes time to make a shorter cast.

In addition to stripping the streamer, try jigging the rod tip as the streamer comes back to your position. This could elicit a strike from the trout that might be following your fly. Cover the water thoroughly, ensuring that your flies have been cast into every single likely place that a trout might be. One thing to avoid here is to allow the streamers to swing below your position. We are trying to pull our streamers *toward* the fish, so that the fish will have two choices: to either eat it or move out of the way. When a streamer is swinging or hanging below your position, trout have a tendency to nip at the tail. This results in many short strikes.

When you are fishing streamers from shore, be sure to fish the area very thoroughly. This means that you might have to make more casts than you usually would to elicit a strike from the fish. Let's say that it usually takes you about twenty or so casts in an area to take a fish. During high and stained water, you might have to make fifty casts in order to take the fish. This is mainly due to the fact that the trout are not able to see as well. Slowing down and really methodically covering the water with multiple casts in the same area will pay large dividends in increased catch rates. Simply making a few casts, getting discouraged, and moving on to the next spot does not work during high water. More casts in the right water will be more efficient than fishing multiple areas with fewer casts. This method is extremely similar to prospecting with dry flies.

Before making a cast with streamers, be sure to have the correct amount of line out of your rod. This will result in fewer tangles and more-effective presentations.
DAVE LATTNER

If you need to achieve more depth than what the floating line allows, add VersiTips to your leaders. These are sink tips that range in sink rates from an intermediate all the way down to tips with high sink rates, to get your flies down in even the deepest of pools. This eliminates the need to carry additional spools for additional sinking fly lines. An angler can easily store these sink tips in a leader wallet and quickly change them as needed. This is a very efficient system when fishing larger rivers and streams with lots of variance in depth.

Another way to achieve greater depth when fishing streamers while wading is to stick the tip of the rod in the water, especially effective when using longer sinking tips. This will give you an almost direct connection to the streamer and will also help with the hook set because you are less likely to raise the rod, meaning you're less apt to change the angle of the hook.

Boat-Fishing with Streamers

Fishing out of a boat with streamers is an effective way to cover lots of water. When fishing out of a boat, or "banging the banks," you are able

Fishing out of a driftboat, the author casts directly at structure along the shoreline, hoping to lure out a large trout. DAVE LATTNER

Casting ahead of the boat at a 45-degree angle allows the author's streamers to sink to the correct depth. BOB CARPENTER

to cover miles of stream in a day rather than just hundreds of yards. You are making so many casts that it's not uncommon to get fatigued. Fishing streamers from a boat can also be very exciting. Oftentimes you'll make your cast and see the fish either take your fly or chase it down. This can make for some real adrenaline rushes. The only downside is that you generally get only one chance to make the trout take your streamer. Repeated casting to the same area usually does not entice the same fish out of its lie. When you miss a fish, start false-casting again while looking for the next-best holding lie to cast to.

STREAMER

2' - .021" Powerflex

Perfection Loop

24" to 40", 2 - 0x
fluorocarbon, depending
on water clarity and
current velocity

Nail Knot off the Fly Line

109

When presenting flies to trout from a boat, you generally cast your streamers downstream ahead of the boat at a 45-degree angle. Strip in the fly until it is parallel with the boat, and then recast. You don't want to cast the fly parallel to the boat's position or behind it. Because the boat is moving, your fly will be moving too fast, and you'll have very little control over the movement of the fly. In addition, make sure that you cover all of the "prime" lies. Many anglers will simply employ rapid-fire casting; then, when the "perfect" spot comes along, they aren't ready and will either make a sloppy cast or one that misses the target altogether. When fishing from a boat, make every cast count. It's very rare that you'll get to make a cast in the same place twice.

Tandem Streamers

There are moments when fishing with tandem streamers can be quite productive. Your streamers can be either unweighted or weighted, depending on the water type. If the flies are weighted, this could

The author is casting streamers at the bank. It is clear that the rod is held low near the water's surface. Additionally, the spray is coming off the fly line, which indicates a quick erratic retrieve—hopefully enticing a trout to take his offering. DAVE LATTNER

possibly eliminate the need for a sinking line. Remember: Most of the time when you're fishing streamers, whether from a boat or wading, you are casting into fairly shallow water. The majority of the fish are found in depths of one to three feet. Only under certain circumstances are the trout found in extremely deep water. Although the fish might be deeper, it is often difficult to put your flies at those depths, either because of the moving boat or, when wade-fishing, because of the angles at which you are casting.

One simple way to achieve more depth is to make an upstream mend and feed out a few feet of line after making your cast. This will give your flies a chance to sink. Be cautious when doing this with sinking lines, however; if the line is too heavy, your flies could get snagged on the bottom. If you are fishing tandem streamers out of a boat, a sinking line is often necessary to get your flies down to where the fish are, due to the boat moving as you are retrieving your flies.

Rigging Up to Fish Tandem Streamers

Use a level leader of 2X Fluoroflex Plus tied directly to the end of the fly line. The water depth determines the length of the leader when fishing with a floating line. When using a sinking line, you want to use a shorter leader to ensure that your flies are at the same depth as your line. When using a floating line, make the leader length approximately three times the water depth. If the water depth is eighteen inches, use a length of approximately five feet to the first streamer.

Next, surgeon's-knot a piece of 2X Fluoroflex Plus of about three feet onto the existing leader section. Tie your first streamer to the tag end (created by the surgeon's knot) of the line facing downstream. The second streamer will be tied to the end of the leader, or the point position. Using a level leader helps to cut down on tippet drag in the heavy surface currents, which will aid in keeping your streamers down near the streambed, even as you are stripping them toward you. This is important, because every time you take in line, the streamers are lifted off the bottom. When you pause, they descend again. It's not until they reach the rod tip that they come near the surface. By using the level

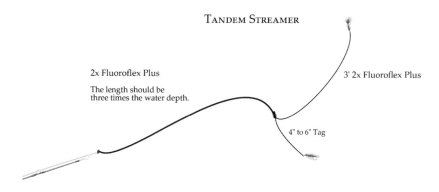

TANDEM STREAMER

2x Fluoroflex Plus

The length should be
three times the water depth.

3' 2x Fluoroflex Plus

4" to 6" Tag

leader, you are keeping your offering in the zone for an extended period of time.

When choosing the streamers that you are going to be fishing in tandem, be sure that the first streamer is larger than the trailing one. Quite often a fish will chase the larger streamer, refuse it, and then take the smaller streamer.

CHAPTER 8

Wet Flies

I can remember when I was young and new to fly fishing, dutifully following my grandfather around the trout streams of Pennsylvania, New York, and New Jersey. Occasionally we would come across a wet-fly angler on the stream. Being inquisitive to a fault, as most youngsters

This nice rainbow took a soft hackle pattern fished in a shallow, low-gradient riffle.
JUSTIN IDE

that age are, I asked my grandpa about this technique, which he had never showed me.

He said, "Aaron, wet-fly fishermen work very hard at their craft, but honestly, they don't usually have much success." When I was younger, my grandfather's word was gospel; that's all I needed to hear. I stayed away from wet-fly fishing like the plague for many years—that is, until I met arguably the most knowledgeable wet-fly fisherman on the planet, Davy Wotton.

Davy is a Welshman, transplanted to the White River in Arkansas. He still maintains that strong and engaging British accent and has also remained dedicated to his fly-fishing roots in the United Kingdom. Davy is the originator of many of the fly-tying products we enjoy today, including Wapsi's "Synthetic Living Fiber" dubbing blends. His Davy Wotton fly knot, which he created during his earlier angling days, is in my opinion the simplest and most functional fly-attaching knot in use today, especially for smaller flies. As one very prominent Montana fly-fishing educator and outfitter once said to me, "Davy Wotton is the

This average-size trout was caught on a large wet fly. When the sun goes down, the average size of the trout goes up. This is generally true no matter where you fish in moving water. HEATH POTTER

guy I call whenever I need to confer with someone about anything fly fishing–related."

I was fortunate to learn a great deal about wet flies from Davy Wotton, spending many days on the river with him. I can assure any angler that catching trophy-size trout on wet flies is not a rare occurrence for him.

Wet-fly fishing arguably originated in the British Isles over four hundred years ago. American wet-fly techniques have typically consisted of a down-and-across presentation. We strip in the sunken fly with a huge belly in our line, usually with limited success. In traditional UK techniques, the "cast of flies" is presented in such a way as to place the offering at several different positions in the water column and in all quadrants of the stream. The top dropper can actually present above the meniscus, while the middle dropper presents as the emergent stage, and the anchor fly, at deeper levels in the water column, as possibly some sort of nymphal form or other food source. I was fortunate to learn what flies to use and where on the cast the flies should be placed.

On one of Davy's trips east I took him to the Neversink River in the Catskills. This area is considered by some to be the birthplace of American fly fishing. On the way up I described that we might expect some finicky, surface-feeding trout. We were going to arrive in late afternoon. He announced that he intended to employ wet-fly techniques and that he would entice some trout even if they were not in the mood by working the flies and animating them throughout the drift. He went on to tell me that even during a heavy hatch, wet flies fished below the hatch can often produce the best results. He continued to say that even when the sun is high in the middle of the day, one could catch good numbers of fish. He said it's a very active method, which strives to induce an instinctive reaction from the fish. Your flies tell the fish, "I'm food, I'm alive, and I'm attempting to get away."

Davy was right that day on the Neversink. The dry-fly fishing was nothing to write home about, and on the ride back, I had to endure Davy talking about how he "cleaned my clock" wet-fly fishing. I learned a lot that day.

Tackle and Lines

The animation, or the way in which you work the flies, is key to fishing a team of flies. Your animation of the flies is helped by the use of a ten- to eleven-foot, mid-flex rod. The rod needs a very flexible tip section, which helps give action to the flies. The fly lines of choice are either a Trout LT weight-forward or a double-taper, depending on the conditions. A weight-forward line helps on windy days, while the double-taper works well when there is no wind. Additionally, an Aqualux intermediate sinking line is perfect for windy days, when keeping your flies in position is essential. (This will be discussed in detail later, on page 129.)

By working the cast of flies during the drift, one can make them appear as though they are either swept up in the current, emerging, caught in the film, hatching, spent on the surface, or even diving like an egg-laying caddis. Davy likes to give the trout as many reasons as possible to accept the presentation.

When you are using the proper tackle, the cast of flies is laid out in a straight line and you can fish the flies more effectively.

The author demonstrates the perfect angle for fishing wet flies. The 45-degree angle is essential, as is the angle at which the line hangs off the rod. This is what you want to see when fishing wet flies in any manner. JUSTIN IDE

Rigging

In rigging wet flies, it's important to balance the cast of flies out. The angler has to be able to turn these flies over during the cast. Paying attention to the rigging of your leader system will greatly enhance your ultimate experience with wet-fly fishing.

Most of the time I choose to use three flies in my leader system. However, there are times (perhaps due to regulation restrictions) when you may be required to use only one or two flies. If this is the case, you can pinch on, for example, a number-one split shot above a knot at the terminal end of the leader, about twenty inches from the single dropper. This shot will act as an anchor.

WET-FLY LEADER

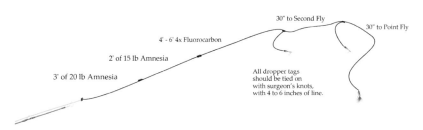

An angler only needs to use a couple of different knots in the system; the emphasis instead should be on leader and dropper lengths. To ensure good movement of the flies, the dropper usually needs to be four to six inches, though the top dropper may at times be increased to as much as ten inches to accommodate what you are trying to do in the film, or the surface, of the water. At times you want the dropper flies to dap on the surface, like a natural insect trying to fly away. Other times you need the dropper to stay in the surface film. The distance from the fly line to the top dropper is four to six feet of 4X to 5X Fluoroflex Plus.

When fishing wet flies on a floating line during upstream presentation, an angler might want to increase the distance to the first fly to as much as six feet from the butt section of the leader. For the butt section of my leader, I like to use three feet of twenty-pound Amnesia tied with a surgeon's knot to fifteen-pound Amnesia. You can use either red or fluorescent yellow for this section. The high visibility of the material aids in detecting strikes and letting you know when to mend your line. For across-stream presentations, four feet from the butt section to the top dropper is all that may be needed. For sunken- or intermediate-line techniques, the rule of thumb is four feet of Fluoroflex Plus as well. This is important, because you can work the top dropper and detect strikes more effectively.

From the top dropper knot to the middle dropper knot, you want to space the flies between twenty to thirty inches apart. It's important to keep the spacing of these knots the same in relation to the terminal end of the leader. If using across-stream, dead-drift techniques, you want this spacing to be thirty inches. Make sure that all of the distances between your flies are equal. According to Davy Wotton, this is how to get the leader system to balance out, to avoid tangles during the casting, and to get the dropper flies to hang on the leader system with the hook point facing out.

When fishing wet flies, you have to pay attention to detail; all of the little things matter. Tippet diameter, for instance. When fishing with size 16 to 18 soft hackles, use a 6X tippet. When fishing sizes 8 to 12 soft hackles and wet flies, use 4X to 5X. When fishing sizes 12 to 14 flies, whether soft hackles or wets, use 4X to 5X as well. When fishing wets and soft hackles in sizes 16 to 20, use 5X to 6X. At times, especially when using flies that are a size 20, I will often use 7X. This will aid in my flies getting down to the fish and will let the flies act more naturally. My tippet when using wet flies and soft hackle is always Fluoroflex Plus.

Fly Selection

Fly choice and position, when fishing soft hackles and wet flies, are unusually important, especially when compared to other forms of subsurface fishing. The cast of wet flies that I was taught by Davy seems to work together as a team. Each fly has a position and a

This nice wild brown trout was taken on a flymph—a fly that can either be fished wet fly–style or nymphed. JUSTIN IDE

function and adds to the overall presentation. For most wet-fly fishing, you will generally be fishing with three flies in a setup. These flies consist of an anchor fly or tail fly, which is at the point, or end, of the rig. This is usually an attractor pattern, tied with a little more bulk. Many of these patterns are tied on a heavy hook and are fished deeper in the water column, serving as an anchor for the rest of the flies in the setup. The middle dropper is a deceiver and usually depicts an emergent bug of some sort. This is where you tie in the fly that you want to closely imitate the insects that are swimming to the surface to hatch. Finally, the top dropper should be an imitation of an insect. It is usually taken as an emerger or dun. This could be a winged wet fly, or even a dry fly. This fly often has wings and can be taken as either a cripple, which is attempting to leave the surface of the water, or a dry fly dapping the surface in preparation for a short flight to streamside vegetation.

119

In this box of soft hackles, note that there are many generic patterns. You do not need a selection as varied as this, although a good assortment of hare's-ear soft hackles in various sizes is important. SIMON GAWESWORTH

Conditions such as light and time of day can influence your choice of flies. Generally there are certain flies which work better at a given position on a three-fly setup.

For the tail or anchor fly, use attractors that have colors the fish will readily see and hopefully react positively to. Some flies that work best in this position are an Alexandria, Peter Ross, or a Silver Invicta. Each of these wet flies are colorful and have tinsel bodies to flash and attract the trout's attention.

For the middle dropper Davy Wotton recommends a deceiver. Deceivers contain some elements of a natural insect. Some middle dropper suggestions are an Invicta, Winged Wet Hare's Ear, Partridge and Yellow, Cinnamon Gold, and the Poacher.

An angler wants the top dropper to move up the water column from a given depth. As a rule of thumb, Davy suggests a light fly for a light day and a dark fly for a dark day. Some suggestions for the top dropper are Muddler Daddy, Palmered Grenadier, Invicta, and Palmered

Coch-y-Bondhu. Most of these flies contain a lot of material, such as a palmered body, which enables them to be fished right in the surface film. Fishing caddis dry flies on the top dropper during a caddis hatch can lead to some excellent results, especially during heavy insect emergences. A couple favorites are a Henryville Special and an X-Caddis.

Soft hackles fish better when dead-drifted; they are not designed to be cast across-stream or to have motion imparted when fishing them. These are some of the best imitation of emergers available. Typical soft hackles which Davy uses are Partridge and Olive, Purple and Snipe, Usk Nailer, Partridge and Pheasant Tail, Hare's Ear Soft Hackle, and Grouse and Copper.

Upstream Presentation

Davy employs an upstream presentation when fish are feeding high in the water column. This works exceptionally well when trout are found actively feeding and can be seen occasionally taking insects from the water's surface. An upstream presentation is also beneficial because the angler is less apt to spook the fish when approaching them from behind.

Here the author presents wet flies upstream of his position. This tactic is deadly on actively feeding trout. JUSTIN IDE

In addition, there is a greater potential for a solid hookup. When setting the hook, you are pulling the fly back into the fish's mouth.

Often when you think the fish are feeding on the surface, they are really feeding on insects in the surface film, or slightly below. Although the trout's scope of vision is precise right up to the surface, they are not able to see as well above the surface. Interestingly, it can take insects just milliseconds to complete the hatching process right at the surface. Trout will often key in on one stage and eat only that. For this type of situation I recommend imitative flies in sizes 14, 16, 18, or even all the way down to a 20, depending on the size of the naturals. Weighted flies are not ideal for this technique, due to the fact that the trout are feeding so close to the surface. If you need to fish your flies at depth, make the switch to an intermediate line.

When fishing upstream with soft hackles and wet flies, make short casts upstream and slightly off to the side of your position. Once the cast is made, raise the rod tip as soon as the flies make contact with the water. This will help you to gain contact and control all the way down to the tail fly. As the flies drift, follow them with your rod tip and keep a consistent belly in your line. At the end of the drift, fish the flies down and past your position and, once downstream, let them dangle for a little bit. Occasionally a fish will take your flies at the end of the drift, as the flies ascend to the surface. Once you have covered all the water at that distance, wade upstream just the length of your rod. Do not make big changes in position. Be sure you cover all of the water in a given area before moving on. Do not lengthen your casts. Just reposition yourself slightly upstream in approximately ten-foot increments. When approaching a section of water, always work the closest water first. Don't wade through possible good holding water along the edge.

Remember that upstream wet-fly and soft-hackle fishing generally means a short line and a dead-drift presentation.

Across-Stream Presentation

When presenting across-stream, a double-tapered line is best. Keep the length of the line at about one or two rods' length. Make your cast

The author fishes wet flies up and slightly across from his position. You can see that the rod is at a 45-degree angle and the flies are dead-drifting past his position. JUSTIN IDE

slightly up and across at a 45-degree angle, and then dead-drift the flies. Keep the rod fairly low after the delivery of the flies.

After making the cast, dead-drift the flies until the current influences them. At that point, make a slight rod mend upstream. This slows down the flies and puts you in contact with them. Track and work the flies into likely current seams. Animate your flies with a slight twitch of the rod tip. When the flies are downstream, mend and twitch to bring the flies to life while on the "dangle."

When making this presentation, do not lengthen the cast. Instead, wade a leader's length upstream, or possibly downstream, to cover new water. Keep the rod at a 45-degree angle as the flies drift along with the current. As the flies come across your position, raise your rod tip slightly up. This is somewhat like a mend. It allows your flies to hang and dangle in the current and slows their drift once the swing starts, allowing you to extend the drift to below your position.

As the flies move downstream, you can control the speed at which your flies track down and back toward the angler's side. To slow the

123

swing, move the rod up; to speed up the swing, move the rod downstream. Simply changing the rod angles will change how the flies are fished. It might be necessary to do this several times, even during the same cast. In a situation where you need a longer cast that requires fly line on the surface, try your best not to allow the line to move back over the fish before the presentation reaches them. For this reason, keep the fly line slightly off to the side of where the fish might be holding, avoiding the possibility of spooking the fish with your line. As the flies move downstream, you can sometimes raise your rod to impart a slight turn-around movement, which can elicit a strike.

The leader length, including the butt section and three flies, can range from fifteen to eighteen feet in length. The strategy for the across-stream technique is the same as the upstream presentation. Exhaust the quadrant and then move up three or four yards. Do not make too long a movement upstream, as you might pass up a piece of water that holds fish. In addition, watch the top dropper fly like a hawk; it may indicate

The author is about to net a nice wild brown that took a winged wet fly on an upstream presentation. JUSTIN IDE

a strike below. And if you have soft hackled flies in your cast, remember that by design, they are not meant to be dragged across the current at high rates of speed.

Down-and-Across Presentation

This presentation is used when the angler feels the trout are keying on emergers. It's an extended presentation, and you will want to use a dry-fly line so you can work the flies in the surface film. After the cast you want to employ a slow, continuous retrieve. It's important to learn how to perform a hand-twist or figure-eight retrieve in order to be able to control the slack line as the flies are drifting. This simple retrieve is done by taking in line with your pointer finger and making loops in the palm of your hand with the fly line. This aids in keeping the line out of the water, giving you more control. It takes some practice to become proficient at this. I suggest that you practice it at home in front of the TV. This retrieve, combined with the movement of the rod (held at a 45-degree angle), is key to the down-and-across presentation.

Here you can see the 45-degree rod angle, as well as the perfect angle at which the line should come off of the rod tip during the down-and-across presentation.
JUSTIN IDE

Fishing wet flies down and across accounted for this hookup with a nice trout.
JUSTIN IDE

A standard butt section is used with this rig. After the butt section, tie a four- to six-foot leader section of Fluoroflex Plus to the butt section, and then tie in the top dropper. To that, tie in two thirty-inch sections of Fluoroflex Plus of the same diameter. Remember to match the tippet diameter to the hook size. When fishing surface techniques, you might want to make the midsection a bit longer. The overall length of the leader should be twelve to fourteen feet.

Typical flies to choose for this technique might be Invicta for the top fly, a soft hackle for the mid-position, and possibly a hare's ear with hackle as the tail fly. This hackle body tends to help hold the cast of flies in position during the drift. It's important to note that this technique works best when using a mid-flex action rod. You need good rod-tip flexibility in order to impart the appropriate movement on the flies.

The cast is made across-stream, and then a quick line mend is made upstream. This is different than the rod mend described earlier. This particular line mend helps to slow the flies down as they come across and eliminates any adverse drag. Work the flies slowly near the surface using the figure-eight retrieve and additional line mends as needed. After the flies have moved across stream to below your position, you should pick the flies up very slowly; oftentimes, this can elicit a take at the end of the drift.

When comparing this with the typical American technique, one can readily see the advantage of this method for across-stream application. It gives the fish more time to take a look at the flies and allows the flies to move through the fish's feeding environment in a more-natural way.

I have always said that I would rather have good presentation technique than the best flies. I was having a good day wet-fly-fishing using Davy's across-stream technique. My friend Bob and I were on the Ruby River in Montana, and he challenged me to use one of his flies to see if I would have as much success. I accepted the challenge, which would determine who was going to pay for dinner that night. With a smirk he pulled out the absolute gaudiest wet fly I had ever seen. He called it "the Skunk." Bob's intermediate status as a fly tier made it even more of a challenge. Needless to say, after I employed the proper across-stream presentation, Bob's wallet came out when the check arrived that

Here the author is hooked up to a nice trout in a shallow riffle after using a down-and-across wet-fly presentation. Shallow, riffled water begs for a wet-fly presentation, especially in areas where there are no obvious current seams. JUSTIN IDE

evening. Besides providing me with a free steak dinner, the real benefit I've reaped from this presentation is discovering that it works well high in the water column, when you suspect insect and fish activity. Casting your flies across and slightly upstream can often bring great rewards.

After casting, make an immediate upstream mend. Because of the minimal time for a dead drift, you should raise the rod tip right away and follow the flies to achieve the longest drag-free drift possible. Once the flies are below you at a 45-degree angle, you should work the flies and track them. While doing this, manipulate the flies with the rod tip and "dance" them into various seams. Recover the flies even when they have swung to the end of the drift. Use slight hesitations with the retrieve, allowing them to fully fish the "dangle" at the end of the drift and during the retrieve.

The key here is to track and animate the flies while you recover them with the hand retrieve. It's important to understand that wet flies should not be stripped in at the end of the drift. In addition to the figure-eight retrieve, Davy also demonstrates the open-loop retrieve and the twitch retrieve. The *open-loop retrieve* is used in slower-moving water and involves collecting loose loops with the non-rod hand while holding the line against the rod

At the end of your cast, lift the rod up and impart motion with the rod tip while using the figure-eight retrieve. JUSTIN IDE

with the rod-hand index finger. He combines this open-loop retrieve with the figure-eight / hand-twist retrieve. The *twitch retrieve* starts with the little finger of the rod hand holding the line while imparting a short twitch retrieve with the first two fingers of the non-rod hand. These line-recovery techniques are an integral component of the system, providing, along with various rod movements, the means to animate the flies.

It's important to emphasize the role of rod position in animating the flies. If the rod tip is kept close to the surface of the water, the movement of the flies during the recovery is very direct and enables the line to instantly "kick" during the recovery. When the rod is held high, the weight of the fly line causes an additional movement during the retrieve. It's like a delayed extra motion. As the line is kicked up, the weight of the line sags, thus pulling on the flies in a secondary, delayed motion. Work them while imparting action as you bring them toward your position for another cast. These retrieval techniques in various combinations can provide a multitude of options for the angler. Rod position in conjunction with varied retrieval techniques will give the fish several different looks to the flies, one of which is sure to induce a take.

It can be tempting to go directly to the extended, across-stream presentation, but I suggest starting with the short-line, across-stream presentation. This will enable you to develop the skills necessary to stay in contact with your cast of flies. Keep in mind that it's always much more difficult to manage a proper presentation when more line is placed on the water. Less is often more when employing this presentation.

When to Use a Floating or Intermediate Line

A floating or intermediate line is recommended when it's windy or when the angler is fishing swifter current. An intermediate line, as the name suggests, is an alternative to a floating or a full-sinking line. A typical sink rate for this type of line would be one to two inches per second. This line density allows the rig to bite in slightly below the surface, thus allowing the angler to "hang" the flies and work them. If you were to use a floating line under these conditions, the flies would tend to skate across the surface. To prevent this from happening, you might try to raise your rod tip up high to lift the line off the water. Under windy conditions this might not be your best option.

Aside from being an awesome fly fisherman, my grandpa was also a mathematician (sarcasm). He taught me this equation: Dry fly line plus wind equals an ugly situation. An intermediate line allows you to set your line down into the current below the film so you can work the flies as they hang in the water column. Note that when making your leader, the distance from the line to the top dropper may have to be adjusted according to how much line you intend to cast. This depends in large part on your on-stream situation the day you're fishing. A good rule of thumb: The longer the line you cast, the greater the distance you want between the end of the line and the top dropper.

The cast is made across and slightly upstream. As soon as the flies hit the water, raise the rod tip high. The intermediate line, by biting in, provides the counter-resistance you need to perform this lifting-rod action. The bow in the line created by this rod action serves as an indicator of sorts. By watching the "angle of hang," we can determine how the cast of flies are being fished and also, ultimately, detect a take. Track the movement of the flies and manipulate them throughout the drift with the tip of the rod. By the way, while all of these things are going on, don't forget to perform a continuous retrieve throughout the drift.

Davy demonstrates two different rod manipulations which can alter the way the flies track through the drift. The first one causes the flies to move downstream and across in somewhat of a U-shape configuration. To impart this action, raise the rod immediately as described above and track the flies downstream while employing a continuous retrieve. This allows the presentation to move initially downstream, the cast of flies to straighten, and the whole rig to move back toward you.

The second rod movement allows you to work the flies downstream in a straight-line angle, across and down. This subtle variation in rod movement can provide a totally different look to the fish. To accomplish this drift movement, lift the rod tip up and slightly to the upstream side. This enables the flies to track less like a pendulum and more in a straight line, across and down. Again, a continuous retrieval is advised throughout the drift.

CHAPTER 9

Fly-Fishing Still Water

Introduction

Fly-fishing in lakes and reservoirs can be a daunting task. The lack of moving water and obvious holding areas can make it more difficult to locate trout in still water. As a result, most fly fishers do not heavily fish these waters. A productive lake, pond, or reservoir, however, can provide some epic fly fishing.

Lake fishing can be rewarding. These two rainbows were landed simultaneously, each in excess of twenty inches. BRIAN CHAN.

Whether fishing from a boat or wade-fishing, you need to keep your rod tip down at the water and strip your fly in with an erratic retrieve. DAVE LATTNER

There are three very distinct types of lake fisheries that anglers will encounter here in the United States. The first is a "put-and-take" fishery, where the trout are stocked in large quantities for anglers to harvest. These are generally located near high-population centers where the lakes create angling opportunities. Even when gear fishermen harvest most of the stocked trout, some will escape harvest and grow to impressive size. The second type of lake, which is more commonly found in the West and extreme northeastern United States, are fisheries made up of entirely wild fish. The majority of these types of lakes are found in higher elevations where stocking does not occur. In these lakes you are catching mostly indigenous species of fish, such as, out West, various species of cutthroat trout, and, in the East, brook trout. The third type of water, and probably the most popular, is a lake wherein the trout are stocked at small sizes and grow in the lake, becoming very accustomed to the food base of that particular water body.

As previously stated, catching trout in lakes can be a daunting task. Lakes lack the obvious places that trout hold, such as current seams formed

Brian Chan holds up a large, British Columbia rainbow trout. BRIAN CHAN

by rocks and obstructions beneath the water's surface. But learning how to "read" a lake can enable you to experience some amazing fishing.

WHERE TO FIND THE FISH

Lakes do have structure that trout like to position themselves around. Lakes have points, drop-offs, humps, weeds, and other features, which are caused by wind. Learning how these features hold fish can enable you to target a specific area within a lake with a certain degree of confidence that fish are present.

Points or rock outcroppings generally contain fish that are cruising around, looking opportunistically for food. They are constantly moving in and out of this type of structure, so the fishing will vary from red-hot to nothing, even within the same hour. One particular spring I was fishing a nice rock outcropping on Spinney Reservoir in Colorado, using three scuds on a floating line. There were other anglers fishing along the same shoreline. I soon realized that when the anglers fishing beside me started to hook up, the fish were coming my way. Every time this happened, I would either land a fish or at the very least, get a take.

The author casts a midge tip at the shoreline in hopes of catching a cruising brown trout. SAM MARINO

Drop-offs into deeper water are popular places where trout will feed on either emerging insects or opportunistically take other food items suspended throughout the water column. Fishing drop-offs can be quite exciting, especially if you're fishing exceptionally clear water. One particular summer I was fishing the shoreline of Quake Lake in Montana. The Callibaetis were hatching heavily, and I was fishing an area where the water went from nearly fifteen feet in depth right up to two to four feet. You could see the pods of brown and rainbow trout come up over the shelf, seeking Callibaetis nymphs, emergers, and adults. I was rigged up with a floating line, a long leader tapered to 4X, and two size-14 hare's ear nymphs. I made the casts in front of the fish as they were cruising and hand-twisted the flies in once I'd let them sink. Every time I did this, I would get a take. This same strategy has worked similarly on other lakes throughout the West, as well as lakes here in the Northeast, during the early season, before the lakes warm up and the trout seek cooler water far below the surface.

Choosing to fish in areas where there are depth changes in the lake, such as humps, often produces cruising fish. These fish will frequently stay near these areas because the humps are generally formed by sediment, which grows weeds, which can contain insects, which the trout can feed on. The only downside to this is that depth changes such as these are best fished from a boat, either stationary or drifting.

On Hebgen Lake in Montana, Simon Gawesworth and I found an underwater hump. Every time we passed this area in our boat, we took a fish, usually a rainbow. We have a local lake here in New Jersey called the Monksville Reservoir. Right near the boat launch there is a hump where the water goes from thirty-five feet in depth to just twelve feet. When the trout are first stocked here, many anglers line the boat launch and catch a fair amount of fish. As soon as the fish get too pressured, they go to the hump. You can drift this shallow hump and catch numerous fish. All trout, whether stocked or wild, learn how to adapt and use the various structures found in lakes.

Weed beds are also excellent places to find trout in lakes. The weeds provide a virtual food factory for the fish. Various species of caddis, damselfly, mayfly, and midge/chironomid larvae will seek out these areas, so trout are always found nearby. On lakes such as Montana's Hebgen and Ennis Lakes, where weed beds abound, an angler can predictably find cruising trout. When fishing weeds beds, the rule of thumb is that the rainbow trout will cruise the outside of the weed beds, while brown trout will be found inside the weed beds, sometimes even feeding right in the reeds on the margins of the lake.

If you are angling on the outside of the weed beds, you can fish with three nymphs or less (but check regulations, as they vary). When fishing inside the weed beds, it is a wise choice to fish with only one fly. I learned this lesson the hard way. I was going to fish Ennis Lake, as there are some splendid brown trout in this lake. My friend Davy told me to fish only one nymph, so as not to get tangled up in the weeds. I made the mistake of not listening to him. There were several large brown trout, all in excess of twenty-four inches, visibly cruising the shoreline right in front of me. I cast my three hare's-ear nymphs at the cruising fish. One of them took one of my nymphs, and, as fast as I could get excited, the fish took me into the weeds. When I rowed the boat over in an attempt to catch the fish, I noticed that one of my nymphs was hung up right on top of the weeds and the other two flies were broken off. Needless to say, I only made that mistake once.

Wind is another factor that will dictate where the trout are holding. Wind creates currents on the surface of a lake, much like that of a stream. The more wind, the heavier the surface current. When this happens, trout will position themselves higher in the water column and will often be seen visibly cruising near the surface, against the current created by the wind. This is especially evident on lakes with very clear water. When you have heavy wind conditions, drifting in a boat while using a drogue or sea anchor can produce good results. Being able to cover large amounts of area and presenting your flies to multiple schools of cruising trout can be extremely productive.

Another feature caused by wind on lakes is something called a *wind lane.* Similar to a current seam in a trout stream, this is where ripples from the wind meet a patch of flat, calm water. Food items often get blown to these spots and drop through the water column. Locating these areas can produce excellent results, especially on lakes with holdover and wild trout populations. I will never forget one particular day on Hebgen Lake. The wind was variable, and there was no constant wind creating surface current. However, every time one of these wind-created current seams appeared, my friend told me to make a cast right on the current seam, and nearly every time, a trout took my fly.

Food Items

The food web in lakes is not as varied as in a fluvial environment. There are several species of caddisflies, various mayflies, damsel flies, and chironomids (or midges). Although you can carry thousands of fly patterns with you, fly selection for lake fishing can be streamlined to just a few items. In every good lake angler's fly box, you will see an assortment of chironomids in sizes 10 to 16 (larger than for rivers), hare's-ear nymphs, Diawl Bachs, and various damselfly patterns. For the chironomids, black, red, orange, olive, and claret cover the majority of colors. If you were to carry a basic assortment of these flies with you on a trip to a

Notice the number of slim chironomids in this properly stocked lake fly box.
BRIAN CHAN

lake, you'd likely have all the flies you'd need. The only time that it helps to be more particular is when the trout are feeding up on the surface; it's here that you'll need to match the naturals more closely.

Tackle and Lines

Fly-fishing in lakes generally requires a six- to a seven-weight fly rod, nine and a half or ten feet long—although eleven-foot rods can come in handy at times, especially when nymphing and wet-fly fishing. The ideal weight of the rod depends on multiple factors. If you're fishing a lake with larger fish and using heavier tippet material, you would want to go with a seven-weight. If you're fishing for smaller fish, a six-weight might be more practical. Indeed, a six-weight is the better all-around choice for lake fishing. In addition to fish size, the amount of wind on a lake on any given day will dictate the size of rod that you might choose to use. If there is heavy wind, a seven-weight rod will enable you to cast more efficiently, placing the flies where you need them to go. On a day where the lake is flat calm, a six-weight rod might be all you need.

A ten-foot, six-weight, fast-action rod is the most common choice for North American lake fishing. SAM MARINO

When fishing lakes, your line is the most critical piece of tackle. The line helps you to get your flies down to the level where the fish are feeding. Many lake anglers I know will carry up to sixteen different lines with them. For my part, I've streamlined my list to the following five line types: a double-taper floating line; an intermediate sink-tip line; and RIO's InTouch Type 3, 5, and 7, full-sinking lines. If you have these five lines, you'll be prepared for almost any lake-fishing situation.

A *double-taper floating line* is the line of choice when fishing surface flies, as well as for fish cruising just beneath the surface. A double-taper is easier to pick up than a weight-forward line. This is due to the lack of a heavy front taper, which makes it more difficult to make the quick casts that are sometimes necessary, especially when fishing with dry flies. When fishing on the surface of the lake, you are generally casting to fish that are cruising around, picking up food items off the surface. Often you'll have to make a number of casts in order to properly present your flies in front of the cruising fish. Having a line to pick up and recast quickly is essential for these situations.

A wide variety of lines is necessary to be able to fish at the range of depths in which trout travel in lakes. SAM MARINO

This same principle also applies to fishing in wind lanes, where you are usually casting nymphs near the surface. This means you need to keep recasting in order to keep the flies near the seam where calm water meets choppy. This fly line also performs well when fishing wet flies to fish cruising around the margins of the lake. When fishing dry flies to rising fish, a drab-colored line is preferred. Due to the lack of current, a brightly colored fly line has the potential to spook fish. When fishing nymphs with a floating line, however, I prefer one that is more visible. In this case, the line acts almost as a strike indicator. Watching how the line acts as you are fishing the flies is key. A take can be as simple as the line darting out six inches. This is your indication that a trout has taken your flies. Other times the line will dart right out from your position. A floating line is all that is needed to fish your nymphs when the lake is flat calm due to lack of wind.

If there is a slight wind, use a midge tip. This intermediate tip will keep your flies under the surface, and the tip of the line will act as an anchor to keep the wind from moving your flies around beneath the surface. The midge tip comes with a bright yellow running line that acts as a strike indicator. This will keep your flies at the same depth as the

139

The author uses mini lures to fish for stocked trout on a sinking fly line. As you can see by his smile, lake fishing can be as satisfying as river angling. SAM MARINO

floating line. This line is used to fish subsurface flies if there is wind and you need to be able to control where the flies are; otherwise, the wind would move the floating fly line around, creating slack in your line and, as a result, missed strikes.

An *intermediate sink-tip line* allows you to fish subsurface flies, such as nymphs and chironomids and midge larvae, and is especially effective when damselflies are active along the weed beds of a lake. As they make their way to the margins of the lake to hatch, they can often be found swimming near the surface. An intermediate line also gives you the ability to fish streamers (mini lures, as many lake anglers call them). It's effective for fishing nymphs at a greater depth than you can with the floating lines and midge tip. Control the depth by counting the seconds as the line sinks. These lines usually sink between two to three inches per second. If you fish your flies for thirty seconds, the flies will be anywhere from seven to eight feet below the surface. This is something that you have to test out when fishing. When you get the depth right, remember the count. You will often catch multiple fish at the same depth.

In addition to fishing nymphs with this line, you can also fish streamers. This line is perfect for the early season, when fish are found in shallow water and achieving depth is not necessary to catch them. However, if you need your flies to achieve a little more depth, simply make your cast and count as needed to achieve the desired depth. Keep in mind that if you are to retrieve the streamers rapidly with this line, you will lose depth quickly, as the belly of the line does not sink fast enough to keep your flies at a constant depth.

A *Type 3 full-sinking line* is a great streamer line when either you need to fish deep with a slow retrieve or the trout are shallow and a faster retrieve is needed. You can fish your streamers at depths of over ten feet with this line, provided you are not retrieving fast. If your retrieve is quick, your flies will be fishing at a depth between four and six feet. Where your flies are fished with this line and the others varies greatly depending upon how quick the retrieve is. This is mainly due to the fact that the quicker you pick up the line, the less time the line has to sink.

A *Type 5 full-sinking line* works very well when trout, particularly stocked trout, are found between ten and fifteen feet and smaller streamers are being used with a quick retrieve. This is the standard line that I like to use when fishing for stocked trout in lakes. It allows me to fish faster retrieves in shallow water and get reaction takes from naïve trout cruising in the shallows, close to shore. This line also allows you to fish in deeper water around structure, with slow to moderate retrieve rates.

A *Type 7 full-sinking line* is used when fishing waters in excess of fifteen feet, where a quick retrieve of the streamer is needed. This line can also be used to fish in shallower water, where an ultra-quick retrieve is useful. This is the line that I will go to on bright, sunny days when the trout seek deep water.

How to Rig Up for Various Scenarios

When fishing streamers, Fluoroflex Plus tippets between 2X and 3X are preferred. Many factors help to determine tippet length, depending upon how you want the streamer to act; these include water temperature, line choice, and type of fish. When using sinking lines for streamer fishing, understand what you want the line to do. Just because you are using sinking lines of various weights, this doesn't always mean that they are going to be used to keep the flies at a particular depth of the lake. If you are using streamers with little to no weight, using a long piece of tippet between the fly line and the fly might actually allow the streamer to have more action. Fishing streamers with a longer piece of tippet, generally between four and five feet, is ideal for those conditions when the water temperature is between 50 and 65 degrees Fahrenheit and the trout are active. When the water temperature falls below this ideal range, you should use a shorter distance between the fly line and the streamer. A shorter leader when combined with a slow retrieve will appeal to these more-lethargic trout. At times you'll find yourself simply swinging the streamers through likely holding water.

Another rule of thumb when fishing streamers in lakes is, the greater the sink rate of the line, the closer you want your streamers to be to the line. When fishing an intermediate line, I will commonly place my first streamer four feet away from the line and space the other streamers

LAKE LEADER

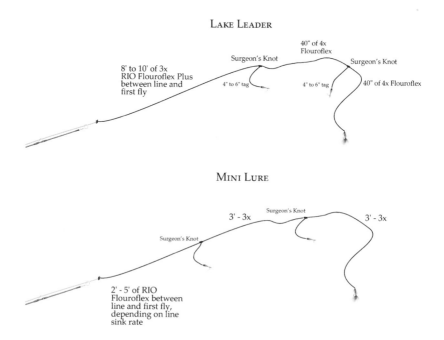

MINI LURE

thirty to forty inches away from the first one. When using a Type 3 line, I cut the distance down to three feet. I keep the distance between the flies constant, as it balances the rig out and reduces tangling. When using Type 5 and Type 7 lines, my first streamer is commonly placed only two feet away from the line. The only adjustment that I might make here is that if the fish are pressured, I will use lighter fluorocarbon and lengthen the distances between the fly line and the first fly. If the water in the lake is extremely clear, the line might be seen by the fish.

Fishing from the Shore

When fishing from the shore, you don't have the luxury of being able to move all over the lake to find fish. The most successful tactic will be to position yourself in an area where there is structure and be patient. Trout in lakes are constantly moving around and should eventually come to the area in which you are fishing, especially if you keep in mind the various structures in which trout are found, such as weed beds and points. Working these areas thoroughly will ensure success. When fishing on larger water bodies, fish these areas for shorter periods of time, as the fish might not be in the area in which you are fishing but instead, hundreds of yards down the shoreline. The only time to vary this methodical approach is when fish are rising. In this scenario, you can stalk the fish individually, much the same as you would when fishing for rising trout during a hatch on a stream.

An assortment of rods rigged up for fishing different methods is essential to successful lake fishing. BRIAN CHAN

Fishing from a Boat

Fishing from a boat is the most effective way to approach lake fishing. A boat allows an angler to be mobile and fish multiple areas by simply rowing or motoring to another area. Again, even when fishing in a boat, you want to target the same areas mentioned earlier. These locations will constantly hold fish.

There are two ways to fish from a boat in a lake: The first is by drifting through an area. The second is fishing stationary, or anchoring up. When drift-fishing in a lake, a drogue or sea anchor will slow the boat up, enabling the boat to float in a straight line and you to make casts without having the boat spin around or move faster than you're able to retrieve the flies. This is the most popular way to fish a lake, especially with competition anglers. It allows you to cover lots of area on every drift, enabling you to present your flies to as many fish as possible.

The second method of fishing from a boat in a lake is to anchor up close to some sort of structure. This is disadvantageous, however, because you are not using the boat to its full potential. You are not able to be as mobile and therefore have to rely on fish being in the area in which you are fishing. Still, there are times when this can be productive, especially when there is heavy insect activity and there are fish repeatedly cruising the same area.

A drogue slows a boat down in windy conditions, giving fly fishers a chance to make presentations ahead of the boat. SAME MARINO

Fishing the Flies

When fishing mini lures and streamers, after you've made your cast and the flies have landed on the water, start counting the seconds as your flies sink. Given that various lines sink at predictable rates, this will help you to know when your flies have reached the desired depth. After you've put your flies in at the appropriate level in the water column, start your retrieve. Keep the rod tip low, or even in the water, when retrieving the flies. This will aid in keeping them at the greatest possible depth.

When retrieving the flies, make short pulls and longer pulls, varying the retrieve. Hesitating and pausing during the retrieve can also elicit strikes from the fish. The InTouch brand of lines have what are called "hang markers" on the line. When the flies get near the boat and you see the marker, raise the rod tip slightly and hold the flies there for ten seconds. After the ten seconds, retrieve the top dropper to the water's surface. Let the flies rest for ten seconds. You will be amazed at the amount of takes you will get as the flies are hanging there. Many fish will follow the flies as you are retrieving them. When the flies are about to reach the surface, the fish will aggressively strike them. This same presentation is effective when fishing damselfly larvae as well.

Wet-fly fishing in lakes is another way to find success, especially when fish are cruising the margins of the lake and feeding on natural

The author is hooked up to a nice trout while fishing chironomids on a midge-tip line in deeper water, adjacent to a weed bed. SAME MARINO

145

insects. When you make the cast, keep the rod at a 45-degree angle, the same way you would if you were fishing on a stream. Use a figure-eight retrieve to bring the flies back toward your position, and as you do, twitch the rod tip to impart action into the flies. Working your flies in this manner can elicit reaction takes from the fish.

Here you can see the figure-eight retrieve. You want to keep the line in the palm of your hand so that when casting, the line doesn't get hung up in your boots. It also makes it easier to control the excess line.
JUSTIN IDE

Before the flies are recast, the hang is very important. Here the author raises the rod to make his nymphs look like they are ascending up through the water column.
SAM MARINO

The author has the first dropper out of the water and is doing the second part of the hang. The nymphs are held in place for up to a minute in some cases. Many times a trout will follow your flies right up to the very end of the cast before taking them.
SAM MARINO

When nymphing in lakes, there are two presentations that need to be understood. The first is a static presentation, for when the lake is flat calm; the other is a presentation for when there is current, caused by the wind or when fishing from a moving boat.

When fishing nymphs statically, simply make the cast and then take in any slack in the line. This will leave the nymphs in the same position. Once the line becomes tight, retrieve the flies with an extremely slow figure-eight retrieve. When the flies reach the end of the cast, use the "hang" method mentioned above (see page 147). When nymphing in still water, the "hang" represents emerging insects.

The only difference when nymphing from a moving boat is that you are taking in the line at a slightly faster rate, retrieving the flies fast enough to keep the fly line in front of you, so as not to allow it to go behind the tip of the fly rod.

One note to make here is that when angling from the shore, the "hang" is not possible. Rather, when you see the hang markers, raise the rod up slightly and wait for a shorter period of time so as to keep your flies from getting hung up on the bottom.

CHAPTER 10

In the Darkness

Introduction

This is the last chapter of the book for a reason. Catching trout at night is not the first thing that a fly angler should attempt. Most appropriately, a fly angler goes through an evolution. Many of us start off fishing

The author crouches intensely, waiting in anticipation for a take. ALEJANDRO GOMEZ

Here is the second-largest trout ever caught by the author—and it was caught at night! This fish was slightly larger than thirty and a half inches and was taken on a size 4 Montreal wet fly. Trout like this are reason enough to deprive yourself of some sleep. TOM WALSH

with nymphs or dries and then branch out to other tactics, such as dry/dropper, streamers, or wet flies. Night-fishing is an advanced tactic and requires lots of skill, patience, and an ability to read the water. It requires a working knowledge of many of the techniques outlined in this book. At times you can be fishing large wet flies, streamers, or even nymphing, especially on smaller streams. When it all comes together, a successful night fisherman can catch some of the biggest trout of his life.

Fly-fishing at night takes a special dedication. It requires sleep deprivation, sometimes in massive quantities, especially if there is a large trout at stake. I have fished at night for many years and thought I knew what I was doing until I met my good friend Tony Scuderi. We fished together a great deal during the day, and I would typically come up on the high end of the fish counts when we finished up. Naturally, when we went out at night, I thought I would show him a thing or two. I was in for a big surprise.

I'll never forget one experience, when Tony and I were fishing the famous Corner Hole on the Housatonic River in Connecticut. We started at about ten p.m. I took the first fish, a nineteen-inch brown, and thought, "This is going to be easy." But then Tony went on to outfish me five to one, making me realize that I needed to learn more about this new facet of fly fishing. One of his trout was a measured, twenty-four-inch brown trout taken on a Woolly Pusher fly. I was humbled, to say the least.

Not too long ago, I was indicator-nymphing during the day on a riffled section of New York's West Branch of the Delaware. I was catching numerous wild rainbow and brown trout. After a while, I hooked what was approximately an eight-inch rainbow. Out of that same riffle came what looked like a dog chasing down a bone. The only difference was that the bone was a rainbow trout, and the dog was a giant brown trout. The trout ripped the rainbow off of my hook and took right off for the safety of its holding lie.

My friend and I went back to that section of the river and night-fished there for the next three weeks, usually rigged up with three large wet flies on a leader tapered down to .013-inch or twenty-pound test. If this fish was going to be hooked, I definitely didn't want to lose it. After three weeks and at least a dozen trips to this single riffle, it finally happened. The trout took my fly. The fight lasted for about five minutes and was a tug-of-war between the fish and me. With the fish in the net, my friend and I measured it as being nearly thirty-one inches.

Night-fishing may not be for the beginning angler, but it's definitely a tactic that, once mastered, could produce the trout of a lifetime.

READING THE WATER AND SCOPING OUT THE SPOTS
What Big Trout Do at Night

Large trout are predators. When they pass the eighteen-inch range, they tend to change their feeding behavior, especially in streams that have abundant minnow and crayfish populations. The largest trout in a stream have lies where they go during the day to seek safety from predators. Their lies could be as obvious as a logjam or just the belly of a large, deep pool—places where it's hard to reach them. Don't get me wrong; there are certainly times during the day when you can catch large trout, but they tend to let their guard down more during periods when there is no light. They feel safer leaving their comfort zone to find food after the sun goes down; that's when they go "on the prowl." Have you ever noticed that when you walk into a stream, you almost always see small baitfish and crawfish right along the margins of the stream? This is Mother Nature's way of protecting them. They are there because it's safe—at least, until it gets dark.

When large trout move around at night, they go to two main areas. They like the shallow water along the banks of a stream and the tailouts of pools. Of course there are exceptions, but these are the places where they find food; as predators, this is where they go.

When choosing a pool to night-fish, it's best to carefully examine it during daylight hours. Look for where the food is. Next, look for a place where a big trout might reside during the day. If there isn't deep water or a logjam or some other structure where the fish can hold and feel safe from other predators—like birds, otters, and, most importantly, us— this area will most likely not hold a large trout. When you are night-fishing, you're trying to catch an apex predator. Trophy trout often hold in large, deep pools with lots of structure where they can hide during non-feeding periods.

Best Times to Night-Fish

Without a doubt, the prime time to night-fish is between the hours of eleven p.m. and two a.m. Trout need to adjust their vision from daylight to darkness. This also allows for the stream to calm down after the fishermen have left following the evening hatch. This is when the fish feel comfortable, moving out from their daytime lies to begin their search for an easy meal.

Full versus New Moons

If I had to choose the best time to be out night-fishing, it would be the two weeks surrounding a new moon. The lack of light makes the fish feel even more comfortable to come out and feed heavily. Over the past seven years I have kept logs, which show that the darker the night, the better the fishing.

This is not to say that you won't catch any fish during a full moon, because you will. However, because of how much light the full moon puts out, the fish don't feel as safe as they do during a new-moon period. Also, the fish will not be as surface-oriented during a full moon. If you're fishing under a full moon, try nymphing, or swinging or dead-drifting streamers on an intermediate sinking line. This will produce fish when more surface-oriented techniques aren't working.

Colors of Flies

For most night-fishing, it's better to fish with darker flies that create a silhouette against the night sky. Since the trout spend most of their time looking up for food, having flies that create contrast against a dark sky tend to work better than lighter-colored flies. Of course there is one exception to this rule: the dreaded full moon.

When fishing during a full moon, consider flies that are white. One would think that with lots of light, a darker fly would create more contrast, but keep in mind that the more light there is, the warier the fish will become. One important thing to remember is that the color white retains its color at depth, so the trout are able to see it even if they are not feeding near the surface.

When Not to Go Night-Fishing

If there were one time *not* to go night-fishing, it would be on a foggy night. In his video, fly-fishing legend Joe Humphreys recommends not going in the fog—although after the fog lifts, the fishing can be quite good.

TECHNIQUES
Streamers on the Swing

Fishing a streamer on the swing, something like the Woolly Pusher, can make for some excellent night-fishing. The fly is sizable and it moves water, as its name suggests. I list it as the first of the four tactics. It's the

The author ties on a large streamer to be fished at night. Notice that this is not a top water fly. When fishing at night, flies that are fished near the surface are far more effective than those fished on top of it. ALEJANDRO GOMEZ

simplest. The presentation is easy and quite effective. Simply quarter your fly downstream and allow it to swing below your position. As the fly swings through the drift, make sure to hold your rod at a 45-degree angle, and follow the fly downstream by rotating your hips.

At the end of the drift, make three one-inch pulls and jig the rod tip slightly after the three small pulls. Do this until the fly reaches your position. You will be surprised by how many trout will follow the fly right to your position before taking it. A strike from a fish at night is often violent and can break some surprisingly heavy leaders. Be ready for it.

Leader

The leader for this style of fishing is very simple and only requires five knots (including the knot used to tie on the fly). You come off of the fly line with two feet of .021-inch Powerflex monofilament. Next, tie in a twenty-inch piece of .019-inch inch Powerflex using a blood knot. The next piece is twenty inches of .015-inch Powerflex. Using a blood knot, attach a three-foot piece of .013-inch Powerflex. This will be your tippet. You read that right: .013-inch, which works out to be twenty-pound test if you are using RIO Powerflex. There is no need to use fluorocarbon tippets and leaders at night.

Dead-Drifting Streamers

The author takes a moment to quietly listen before he enters the water. This is important to do at night, as there might be fish feeding very close to your position. Do not walk in the water before thoroughly acclimating to your surroundings.
ALEJANDRO GOMEZ

What large trout can resist an easy meal? This is a technique that works especially well during poor conditions like a full moon. Use an intermediate sinking line when employing this technique. Since the areas where trout go to feed at night are often flat-bottomed, snagging the bottom isn't much of a concern here. I saw my friend Tony land a twenty-seven-inch brown trout using this technique on the Farmington several years back. Keep your rod tip up at a 45-degree angle (it will act as a shock absorber), and be sure to bring the rod along and rotate your hips the same way as if you were swinging streamers across the stream. If you are too tight to your flies, you will, more often than not, break the fish

STREAMER DEAD DRIFT

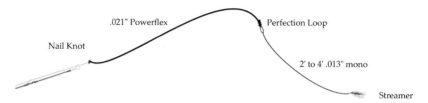

off due to the sudden shock from the vicious take. As you would when swinging streamers near the surface, be sure to slowly retrieve the flies back to your position with short pulls, as well as a slight jigging motion with the rod tip.

Leader

The rigging is ultra-simplistic here. Nail-knot a piece of .021-inch Powerflex monofilament to the end of your intermediate line. Once this is finished, tie a small perfection loop to the end of that. Once you are finished, attach a piece of .013-inch Powerflex. Again, this is going to be the tippet. The most common lengths of tippet are from two to four feet, depending on how deep you want your streamer to drift. A shorter length will keep your fly deeper; a longer length will allow for your fly to ride up slightly off of the bottom.

Nymphing

Nymphing at night when there are stoneflies hatching can be a mind-blowing experience. If you have an area where there is a large brown trout located in close proximity to fast water, you can bet that during the stonefly hatch, this fish will move up into the riffle and feed heavily on stonefly nymphs. When nymphing at night, you'll be fishing a tight-line setup. Since there is no way you'll be able to see the takes, you have to rely largely on feel. The only way to do this is to fish split shot placed between two large dark stonefly nymphs.

This might be the most difficult of all the night-fishing techniques, mainly due to the lack of light. It's hard to see what's going on. The presentation of the flies is as follows: Cast the flies upstream at a 45-degree angle; lead the flies through the drift until they get slightly below your position; then pick them up and recast them. Lead them through the drift, as you want to avoid snagging the bottom. The presentation method is very similar to the Humphreys style of nymphing.

Leader

Nymphing at night, your leader needs to start off with a three-foot piece of .021-inch Powerflex monofilament. Next, attach a two-foot-long piece of .017-inch Powerflex to that. Tie a large tippet ring to the end of the butt section. After tying the butt section, attach a four-foot-long section of 2X tippet to the end of the butt section, using a simple clinch knot to attach it to the tippet ring. To the end of the tippet, tie your first stonefly nymph. Next, tie another two-foot-long piece of 2X to the eye of the first fly. If split shot is needed to reach the bottom of the run, place the split shot halfway up, between the first and second fly.

NIGHT NYMPH

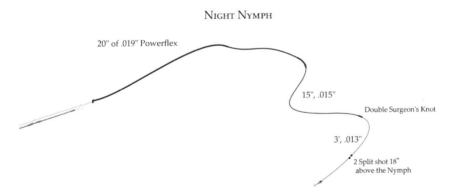

20" of .019" Powerflex

15", .015"

Double Surgeon's Knot

3', .013"

2 Split shot 18" above the Nymph

Swinging Flies

The presentation when you swing flies is the same as when you are swinging streamers. Make a 45-degree cast, follow the flies through the drift, and be sure to keep your rod tip up at a 45-degree angle. As with the streamers, when the flies reach the end of the drift, be sure to make one-inch pulls, then lightly jig the rod tip. This is my favorite way to night-fish, because the takes can be heart-stopping.

When swinging flies, fly selection is not an issue. You can swing almost any fly you want. Traditional wet flies work well, especially the Montreal and the Governor. However, swinging large rubber-legged

When the cast is made, your body needs to be in a position to follow the flies as they swing in the current. The same is true when fishing wet flies. ALEJANDRO GOMEZ

The author rotates his hips and rod to follow the flies as they swing in the current. ALEJANDRO GOMEZ

stoneflies and hellgrammites also works well. There are also times when a combination of two wet flies with a streamer on the point does very well. When swinging flies at night, keep changing flies until you get a tug from that big brown.

When the flies start to reach the end of the drift, the angler should be turned and almost facing downstream. This puts the angler in position to detect a strike and set the hook. ALEJANDRO GOMEZ

Finally, the angler raises the rod tip and retrieves the flies back to his position using a figure-eight retrieve. You never know when the trout will take your flies. ALEJANDRO GOMEZ

Leader

The leader's butt section is very short; it needs to be in order for the series to get down to a smaller-diameter tippet, to tie the flies to. Start off by clinch-knotting a twenty-inch piece of .019-inch Powerflex monofilament. Next, tie in a fifteen-inch piece of .017-inch tippet. To that, tie in a fifteen-inch piece of .015-inch tippet. Up until the end of this section, you are using all blood knots. To the end of the .015-inch tippet, tie in a three-foot piece of .013-inch monofilament, using a surgeon's knot. The first and smallest fly will be tied to the tag end of the knot.

NIGHT SWINGING FLIES

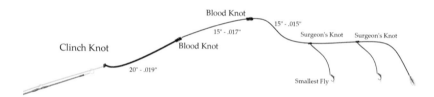

A FEW ESSENTIAL DRY FLIES

Improved Elkhair Caddis

Hook: Regular dry-fly hook, sizes 10 to 18.
Thread: Size 8/0 (70 denier).
Body: Antron dubbing.
Hackle: Dry-fly hackle.
Underwing: Cul de canard.
Wing: Elk or deer hair.

Note: Tie the regular Elkhair Caddis and my Improved Elkhair Caddis in a variety of sizes and colors to match the real adult caddisflies you encounter when fishing.

Blue-Winged Olive

Hook: Regular dry-fly hook, size 16 or 18.
Thread: Olive 8/0 (70 denier).
Tail: Dark-gray hackle fibers.
Body: Olive dry-fly dubbing.
Wings: Gray hackle tips.
Hackle: Gray.

Fan Wing Coachman

Hook: 2X-long dry-fly hook, sizes 12 to 16.
Thread: Brown 8/0 (70 denier).
Tail: Golden pheasant tippet fibers.
Body: Peacock herl and red floss.
Wings: Slips clipped from white duck shoulder feathers.
Hackle: Brown.

A FEW ESSENTIAL NYMPHS AND WET FLIES

Copper John

Hook: Curved-shank scud hook, sizes 14 to 18.
Head: A small or medium gold or copper bead.
Thread: Brown 6/0 (140 denier).
Tail: Brown goose or turkey biots.
Abdomen: Medium copper wire.
Thorax: Peacock herl.
Wing case: Gold Flashabou or Mylar tinsel, and a strip clipped from a turkey tail feather.
Legs: Brown mottled soft hackle fibers.

Big Black Stonefly

Hook: 3X-long nymph hook, sizes 6 to 12.
Thread: Black 6/0 (1240 denier).
Head: Gold bead.
Tail: Turkey biots.
Body: Black dubbing.
Wing case: Slips clipped from a dark turkey feather or a substitute.
Legs: Rubber legs.
Antennae: Turkey biots.
Note: Use black materials to tie an imitation of a black stonefly, or light tan ingredients to make an imitation of a golden stonefly.

Flashback Pheasant-Tail Nymph

Hook: Regular nymph hook, sizes 14 to 18.

Thread: Black 8/0 (70 denier).

Tail, abdomen, thorax, and legs: Pheasant tail fibers.

Rib: Gold wire.

Wing case: Narrow Flashback tinsel or Flashabou.

A FEW ESSENTIAL STREAMERS

Marabou Brown Trout

Hook: 4X- to 6X-long streamer hook, sizes 2 to 10.

Thread: Black 6/0 (140 denier).

Body: Gold braided or flat tinsel.

UnderWing: Yellow and red bucktail.

Wing: Tan or light brown marabou, and gold or holographic gold Flashabou.

Crystal Bugger

Hook: 4X-long streamer hook, sizes 4 to 8.

Thread: Black 6/0 (140 denier).

Head: Gold bead.

Tail: Black marabou and green Krystal Chenille.

Body: Olive Crystal Chenille, hackle, and rubber legs.

EZY Crayfish

Hook: 6X-long streamer hook, sizes 4 to 8.

Thread: Brown 6/0 (140 denier).

Weight: Non-lead wire.

Eyes: Bead-chain or dumbbell eyes.

Claws: Rusty-orange marabou.

Body: Rusty-brown chenille.

Rib: Copper wire.

Shellback: Brown polypropylene yarn.

Hackle: Brown saddle hackle.

Note: Al Beatty developed this great pattern. Big trout and landlocked salmon love to eat crayfish, and they love the EZY Crayfish, too.

INDEX